DEMONIC TO DIVINE

Demonic to Divine

The Double Life of Shulamis Yelin

SHULAMIS YELIN

GILAH YELIN HIRSCH & NANCY MARRELLI

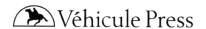 Véhicule Press

Published with the generous assistance of the Canada Council for the Arts, the Canada Book Fund of the Department of Canadian Heritage, and the Société de développement des entreprises culturelles du Québec (SODEC).

Cover design: David Drummond
Typeset in Minion and Bodoni by Simon Garamond
Printed by Marquis Printing Inc.

LIBRARY AND ARCHIVES CANADA CATALOGUING IN PUBLICATION

Yelin, Shulamis, 1913-, author
 emonic to divine : the double life of Shulamis Yelin / Shulamis Yelin,
Gilah Yelin Hirsch, Nancy Marrelli.

Short stories.
Includes bibliographical references.
Issued in print and electronic formats.
ISBN 978-1-55065-383-0 (pbk.). – ISBN 978-1-55065-384-7 (epub)

1. Yelin, Shulamis, 1913-. 2. Yelin, Shulamis, 1913- –Mental health.
3. Authors, Canadian (English)–20th century--Biography. I. Hirsch, Gilah
Yelin, author II. Marrelli, Nancy, author III. Title.

PS8547.E43Z465 2014   C813'.54   C2014-903897-6   C2014-903898-4

Published by Véhicule Press, Montréal, Québec, Canada
www.vehiculepress.com

Distribution in Canada by LitDistCo
www.litdistco.ca

Distributed in the U.S. by Independent Publishers Group
www.ipgbook.com

Printed in Canada on FSC certified paper

Contents

Foreword

LAURENCE J. KIRMAYER

IT IS AN UNEXPECTED PRIVILEGE for me to write these words of introduction to the rich and complex work of Shulamis Yelin brought together in this volume. I first met Shulamis in 1981, when I moved back to Montreal after a sojourn in California. I discovered she lived down the hall from the apartment I had rented on Queen Mary Road. She was sixty-eight years old and a vital presence. We shared a love of poetry and spent many hours discussing writing. Shulamis forcefully argued the case for poetry as I struggled to find a balance between literary aspirations and my career as a researcher and clinician. In 1982 I attended a conference at Council Grove, Kansas and was captivated by a talk on artistic process by a visionary painter, who turned out to be Gilah Yelin Hirsch. We discovered, to our surprise, first, that we were both from Montreal and then, that I knew her mother – and so began a friendship and long colloquy on the nature of art, creativity, woundedness and healing. I think I owe my presence in these pages to this bit of shared history, but I hope I can use the occasion to make some wider connections.

Although the title *Demonic to Divine* alludes to extremities of feeling, and the text gives some inkling of the great darkness with which Shulamis struggled throughout her life, the overarching narrative in this volume, for both Shulamis and Gilah, is very much about the transformative power of art and *poesis* – making living things with words and images. There is much pain in these stories, still more in the excerpts from Shulamis's intimate diary and Gilah's reflections – the pain of separation, rejection, injury, and loss – but also moments of great joy and transcendence.

Shulamis's stories of childhood, built around vivid sensory memories, evoke the world she wanted to live in as much as the one in which she actually did live. With words she built a safe place and a gentle persona that honours family and friends, a particular place and moment in time, but also the larger world of poetry and story and language itself – both Yiddish and English in all their vitality. The stories show how, in the absence of a kind of emotional constancy, engagement with language can become a stabilizing force, a container for some of what is catastrophic and unbearable. But language is also a natural intoxicant or elixir, a potion with which to conjure a world, at once private and public, calm and ecstatic, ordinary and numinous.

Shulamis was visited and sometimes possessed by demons. These demons tortured her – in her diaries she records her anguished howls – but, at times, they also brought her something divine: apophatic speech of a distinctively Jewish kind, words that called out to God, crying into the void like Rabbi Nachman, to bridge the intolerable divide between the mundane and ecstatic. Words jumped like high voltage sparks from the everyday blessings, curses, hopes and fears of Yiddish to the magical language of poetic creation. Of course, there are grave dangers that go with this kind of possession and Shulamis suffered these as well, becoming caught in the energies of psychological inflation, swept up in the grandiosity that allows the poet to climb to the podium and become inhabited by divine madness, mistaking oneself for the word.

Throughout her life, Shulamis experienced the twin poles of ecstasy and abjection: feeling most alive when creating or performing, being the center of attention and receiving recognition for her passion and expressive gifts. But, inevitably, the elation and fulfillment of the moment would be followed by deflation, loneliness and absence, with intense feelings of being ignored, not mattering, being passed over. Though writing is a solitary process, its fruits can be shared in moments of intensely fulfilling communion. Artistic creativity involves both poesis and performance – engagement with the intensely private and personal as well as the public and communal. Writing has this double aspect: allowing a kind of heightened consciousness in the moment of creation that brings its own deep fulfillment and then, when the artist performs publically, the reward of human contact and connection – of receiving recognition from the other who returns the poem's gift or embrace.

What then does it mean to produce art out of suffering? If wounding and suffering make us human, so too does the power of imagination which can transmute the lead of depression to the gold of insight. For Shulamis, artistic creation was not a strategy of denial, drawing a *cordon sanitaire* around her darkest misery or making a desperate escape through the roof of imagination. In her struggle to get others to recognize her passion and her pain, *poesis* was a way to layer the light to allow a flickering realization of something other than the self. Her stories and poems stand clearly as gifts, as realizations of the aspiration to be that other, better self, to transcend anger and anguish and live fully, if only for a moment, embodying a way of being that called forth the same kind of aliveness from others.

Shulamis had a deep and abiding commitment to culture, not only *Yiddishkeit* but also the vivid quilt of multiculturalism. The demons Shulamis stared down in her youth were not only her mother's withdrawal and her own depression (the black dog that has beset so many artists), but the collective demons of anti-Semitism and discrimination. And, with enduring relevance for the generations, her work confronts the particularism of the in-group, tribalism, the feeling of hominess (the *heimliche*) and its perduring contrast with the unfamiliar, the foreign and strange – as in her portraits of the intersecting worlds of Christian and Jew in Montreal in the 1920s and 1930s. In their unique particulars, her stories speak to the essential questions of coexistence, diversity and celebration of differences not from a position of detachment but from a rooted cosmopolitanism – one that recognizes Shakespeare as Other but still claims him as our own. Shulamis's work is testimony to the fact that, in moving most deeply into the intimate, personal and idiosyncratic, the artist reaches the most universal and essentially human. The honey on those Hanukkah pancakes her mother once made was a very particular kind of honey but it is also the very possibility of sweetness.

Montreal, Quebec
August 2014

Shulamis at her daughter's wedding, December 28, 1963.
Jewish Public Library.

Preface

GILAH YELIN HIRSCH

BEING SHULAMIS'S DAUGHTER was not easy. The only child of Shulamis Yelin (Sophie Borodensky) and Ezra Yelin, I was born in Montreal and left when I was seventeen. Despite the decades of geographic distance, Shulamis has been viscerally present throughout my life. As a toddler, I experienced my mother's inventive tenderness, such as when she would leave me her lipstick which carried the scent and colour of the lips that kissed me when she left and on her return. But most of my childhood and adult memories are iterations of highly volatile abuse.

Despite the many years of relentless difficulties, at a rational level and from a very young age I somehow knew that Shulamis was doing the best she could within the limitations of a troubled personality and a life characterized by turmoil and tragedy. Although she experienced persistent emotional disturbance from childhood, multiplied by chronic physical pain beginning in her fifties, I admired the fact that she was, nonetheless, a highly gifted artist, feminist, explorer, adventurer, and delighter in life. I credit Shulamis with making culturally unpopular decisions towards my welfare. Knowing the potentially negative psychological effects of a terribly disturbed mother and invalid father, Shulamis perceived the necessity of my early departure from home, and encouraged it, in order to facilitate my own growth and explorations.

Although we visited annually either in Los Angeles or Montreal, it was not until my mother's death in 2002 that I reconnected to my birth city in more ways than I could have imagined. As executor of my mother's will I had to deconstruct her tapestried environment layered with beauty and substance, an apartment filled helter-skelter with a lifetime's treasure trove of all things multicultural, artful, musical, and literary. I knew that each of these carefully selected and cherished objects carried the zeitgeist and values with which I was raised.

With the help of Brett Hooton, who had been Shulamis's assistant at the time of her death, we set up an office in Montreal in which he organized the documentation of her prodigious life and work. It was a three-year task. The many boxes were then transferred to and housed in the archives of the Montreal Jewish Public Library, fulfilling Shulamis's wishes.

In this process I discovered many unpublished stories and the seventy diaries Shulamis kept from age thirteen – when she first noted, "I have certain 'moods' . . . I am seized with a sad melancholy" – until just days before her death in her 90th year. This cache of public and private work prompted me to consider a posthumous book that would weave stories and diary excerpts together to form a biographical arc to provide a deeper understanding of the writer's life.

I had witnessed Shulamis writing in her diaries from the time I was a child, and throughout my adult life I was the recipient of her telephoned anguish when she mislaid or believed she had lost or been robbed of a diary. My first reading of the diaries was a raw immersion into her unmitigated wretchedness. I learned about shocking events in my own infant life as Shulamis told her unsettling story of motherhood. The diaries document her uncontrollable cruelty, narcissism, paranoia, and abuse of others. They also document how she was perpetually "fuelled by anger," as she often told me. Meanwhile, with "one foot still on the boat" she was writing stories about Jewish immigrant family life characterized by humour, pathos, and loving visions that can easily be transposed to immigrant families universally.

Those who knew her well deeply loved and feared Shulamis. They all have vivid, memorable "Shulamis stories" that cite both her dazzling public talks and presentations and her equally bizarre, often outrageous and cruel behaviour. There was no warning as to whether one would be met by the demonic or the divine aspect of her personality. Although physically distant since I was seventeen years old, as the person closest to her I was frequently the target of her demonic aspect throughout our lives. Yet, as I read the diaries, I was often filled with esteem and love for her. Since I myself had experienced serious injuries from a devastating car accident in 1999, I was deeply empathetic to Shulamis's determination not to be stopped by either her emotional or physical suffering in her pursuit of life and learning.

My admiration for her intrepid sense of adventure and travel grew. She continually strove to conquer her constant physical pain and psychological difficulties, and she kept on going.

Shulamis's first book of stories, *Shulamis: Stories from a Montreal Childhood* (1983), was uplifting, funny, family-friendly, and inspiring. Due to its great success, the book went into several editions, was translated into other languages, and is often read in schools. The diaries, however, reveal a warp and weft of mental illness woven among myriad threads that chronicle the turbulent life of a Montreal writer, poet, and celebrity. Although she was plagued with emotional illness, her creative spirit rose indomitably above her despair to create life-affirming, psychologically sensitive, insightful, and often hilarious literature.

The more I learned of Shulamis's personal hell and simultaneous creative output, the more my admiration and love for this embattled, greatly gifted woman grew. In this way, the purpose of the book was born. Excerpts from the diaries interspersed throughout the book have been chosen to illuminate the great schism between her private and public personas – the sheer horror of her everyday psychic existence, juxtaposed with her professional success captivating the minds of others.

The diaries also attest that despite her lifelong search for clinical relief from her innermost demons, the fledgling field of psychiatry was unable to provide adequate help.

Although I had reservations about publicizing any part of the diaries, Shulamis writes at least five times in the diaries that she wishes and expects them to be read. She often states that the diaries are her true literary legacy. When she entrusted me with her private world, I believe that she not only gave me permission but also charged me to judiciously reveal the information. Once I had absorbed the potentially explosive content, I realized that selected passages could be used to portray the range of Shulamis's personality without violating the privacy of others or creating uncomfortable repercussions in the community.

It is with the greatest respect that I offer a glimpse into my mother's layered full spectrum personality, as well as the kaleidoscopic nature of the creative process. Many gifted creative people are plagued by various degrees of emotional illness. Fortunately, the stigma that had forced secrecy about mental illness during Shulamis's life has been lifted, and now there are diverse therapies that can be helpful in alleviating the kinds of mental and emotional suffering she endured.

I hope this book of selected writings by Shulamis will become a resource – an example of transcendence through creative expression, as well as a celebration of the courageous complexity of a rare and singular woman. I sense that the teacher Shulamis would be grateful to know that her most intimate life's work to overcome her crushing hopelessness, may inspire those who suffer from similarly devastating afflictions.

Despite the many years of difficulties and differences between us, Shulamis and I shared significant values as artists, women, thinkers, and doers. On several occasions, we presented our work at the same conferences. This common vision allowed us to share a spiritual *rapprochement* in her last days, in the intensive care unit of the Montreal General Hospital, when we travelled together in an illusory kingdom that Shulamis described in great detail. At one point in our meandering she asked me, "Have I exceeded my allotted days on earth?"

"No," I assured her, "we all live exactly the right number of days."

"Have I caused anyone else to not live their allotted number of days?" she continued, in a unique expression of understanding her effect on others.

"No, we all have our allotted number of days," I repeated. Shulamis whispered: "We have never been closer."

In the best of outcomes, Shulamis's legacy has become a portion of my destiny, one that I whole-heartedly share with the thousands of people whose lives she touched and with those who she will continue to inspire through her work.

This book would not have been possible without the encouragement, support, engagement, and dedication of friends, old and new. I am deeply grateful to Nancy Marrelli and Simon Dardick of Véhicule Press, Shulamis's first publishers, who not only saw the value of producing a book of this nature, but also participated in its shaping, design, and production from inception. As all the original material is housed in the Montreal Jewish Public Library, Marrelli and Dardick most graciously hosted me in their home during many marathon weeks of work, from 2003 to 2014, and logistically arranged for the

Gilah Yelin Hirsch (left) and Nancy Marrelli working on Shulamis Yelin's
papers at the Jewish Public Library, Montreal.
Photo by Simon Garamond.

diaries to be available in venues where we could spend uninterrupted
days poring over them. Although I had already read and annotated
the diaries by the time I presented the idea, I invited Marrelli to read
the diaries with me and over a period of many visits she came to
fully understand the *extremis* of Shulamis's unfolding life. Our years
of side-by-side and often heart-wrenching work together, focusing
on dramatic emotional material, engendered not only an unusual
collaboration, but also a deep, abiding friendship.

I would like to thank Judy Isherwood of Shoreline Publishing, who I
first approached with the idea of this book. Perceiving that this would
be a larger project than her press could accommodate, Isherwood
suggested that I speak with Véhicule Press and generously relinquished
the rights to Véhicule for this purpose.

Many thanks to Shannon Hodge and Daniela Ansovini, archi-
vists at the Jewish Public Library, who patiently spent many hours
facilitating access to the complex array of Shulamis's archives. Many
thanks, also, to my assistant, Anna West, who helped facilitate this
east-west project.

Special thanks to Brett Hooton, who assiduously ordered the documentation of Shulamis's work to prepare it for the Jewish Public Library, and to Judith Lermer Crawley for her many photographs of Shulamis in her later life. I would like to extend my gratitude to Dorland Mountain Arts Colony, where I was granted a six-week residency in 2003 to read and annotate Shulamis's diaries; and to California State University, Dominguez Hills, for a travel grant that aided the completion of this project.

I also wish to thank the many new and old friends who personally welcomed me back to the beautiful and fascinating city of my youth, and who reintroduced me to the treasures and pleasures of Montreal.

And finally, I am most grateful to the Jewish, Anglophone, and Francophone communities of Montreal whose unusual breadth and richness stimulated and supported the life and work of Shulamis Yelin.

Venice, California
August 2014

Preface

NANCY MARRELLI

W ORKING WITH SHULAMIS YELIN and being drawn into her
world was almost always an adventure.

I was pleased to work with her on the manuscript of her first
book of stories, *Shulamis; Stories from a Montreal Childhood*, which
Simon Dardick and I published in 1983. Shulamis grew up in my
neighbourhood, just steps away from where I have lived for most of
my adult life and her stories took me into the world of her childhood
in those streets that were so familiar yet so very different. She was
a wonderful storyteller and that book brought together a moving
and memorable glimpse into her world as the child of immigrant
parents in Montreal. The editing process was complicated but it
went well and the book was a great success. However, Shulamis was
not an easy person to get along with – there were many tensions
after the book was published – and we saw little of each other.

When her daughter Gilah Yelin Hirsch approached us at Véhicule
Press to publish a new collection of Shulamis stories, we were at first
somewhat sceptical. Gilah met with us and explained what she had
discovered in the many diaries she had inherited from her mother.
We agreed that Véhicule Press would proceed with a book. I would
work with Gilah on a manuscript that would include not only stories,
but also selected fragments from the diaries that provide startling
insights into the complexity of this woman who had managed to add
creativity to a life filled with so much mental anguish.

My background as a professional archivist, editor, and publisher
proved to be useful in this project as we pored over decades of documentation (most of it handwritten), selected bits and pieces from
thousands of pages, and pulled it all together into a book with a
very special story to tell.

Our task was not an easy or comfortable one. Reading the diaries
was often painful and shocking. Many times I could only reach out

to Gilah, tears welling as I read the horrific diary entries of her very troubled mother, and wonder how Gilah could have survived such a childhood to become a thoughtful, kind, and gifted artist. It's not surprising that she left home at seventeen and lived so far away from the reach of the darkness that periodically engulfed her mother. The more I read of the anguish so painfully documented in the thousands of diary entries, the more I marvelled that these two women not only survived the horror that touched them both, but that each in her own way overcame it to thrive in her creative life. Shulamis wrote graphically of her debilitating inner agony from a very early age and the diaries witness her increasing paranoia and emotional dysfunction. The diaries also document the serious car accident in 1969 and the ensuing constant physical pain that was part of her suffering until her death in 2002. I came to marvel at the person who wrote those diaries: how she could possibly function in the world (never mind manage to support her family after her husband became disabled), how she maintained a career as a valued

Nancy and Gilah at work in the publisher's dining room,
on the eleven-year "Shulamis" project.
Photo by Simon Garamond.

Master Teacher, and how she continued to have a rich creative life as a writer, storyteller, and artist. Amazingly, the same woman who wrote these tortured diaries also wrote the beloved childhood stories. Her stories speak to the universal human condition but not to the mental suffering she was experiencing as she wrote them in her later life.

Shulamis left us a many-faceted legacy: childhood stories of great warmth and humour; thousands of students who benefited from her creative and inclusive approaches to teaching; and now through her personal diaries, a glimpse of her private world of mental and emotional pain.

The process of bringing this book together was slow – the project took eleven years of on-and-off effort. Gilah lives in Venice Beach, California; I live in Montreal; the diaries are in Montreal and they are massive as well as difficult to read in so many respects. But over time the three of us – Gilah, Shulamis, and I – worked together to create a book that we think is important. It is a story of personal survival and creativity triumphing over the crippling mental dysfunction that available therapies were unable to address. I am grateful, to both Gilah and Shulamis, to have been invited to participate in a project that opens the door, just a little, into a very private, troubled, and creative life.

The book has three distinct elements. The Shulamis stories present a perspective of the world of the author's childhood. The diary entries document Shulamis's inner life. The narratives are what we have researched and written to provide the background and context of Shulamis's life. Together they reveal a multi-dimensional story about a woman who triumphed over her circumstances.

It's an amazing story and we three invite you to share it in this book.

Montreal, Quebec
August 2014

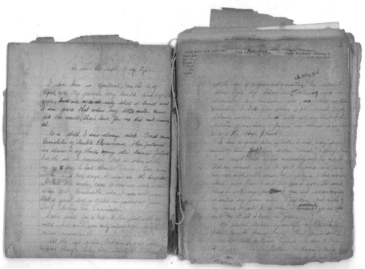

The early diaries.
Jewish Public Library.

The Shulamis Diaries

Sophie Borodensky began her first journal in January 1927 at the age of thirteen. She kept journals sporadically until 1937 when she documented her trip to Russia. We have no surviving journals between 1937 and 1961 and have no reason to believe that she kept journals during that time. From 1961 until her death, Sophie (Shulamis) recorded many aspects of her life in dozens of private notebooks of various sizes and colours. The journals include her struggles with emotional and physical illness, as well as the inceptions and first drafts of almost all her stories and poems. Upon her death, her daughter Gilah was the first person to have access to these notebooks.

Some of her diary entries are interspersed throughout this book with a selection of her creative literary work. There is a stark contrast between the idyllic portrait portrayed in the stories about early childhood, and the growing anguish painstakingly documented in Shulamis's journals. Even the earliest diary entries give clear indications of her troubled inner life, but in contrast, and although they speak to the universal human condition, the stories about childhood betray none of this private pain. Her poetry and some of the stories that touch her adult life portray a more realistic image of the conflicts and difficulties that are also detailed in her later journals.

∾ Diary entry January 19, 1927 [age thirteen]

A Short Biography of My Life
I was born in Montreal, on the 12 of April, 1913. My parents, very lovable and respectable people loved me as an only child is loved and I am sure that when my little sister came into the world, their love for me did not diminish.

As a child I was always sick. First came Bronchitis of Double Pneumonia, then followed an absess [sic] in my throat. Many other

23

diseases followed but the one I remember the best is when, at the age of 4 yrs, I had Scarlet Fever. For nine weeks and two days I was in the hospital, St. Paul. My mother came to visit every day as well as my dear Grandmother, who, I may well say, had a great deal of credit in saving me from Death during the Pneumonia.

I also went for a trip to New York with my mother, but as I was only about 3 yrs. of age, I cannot remember it.

At the age of five I began to go to school. I went through every class steadily and [graduated] at the age of 12 years and 9 months in February 2, 1926. I then entered the Baron Byng High School and continuing my course in education. My continuous wish is to take up medicine. Meanwhile, I have been going to the Jewish Peretz School, which I love with all my heart. I have but one year more to finish my course and have to go to the high school.

I am a great lover of books. I read every spare minute I have but I have certain "moods". Many times I am seized with a sad melancholy and the only thing that can console me is to go to the piano and pour my heart forth to the tunes that I play. I love music much more than I did two years ago. The same thing is with my poetry. I am not as encouraged in writing my poem when I sit down and make up my mind to write it as when I suddenly get an idea and try to set it down on paper.

My Jewish teacher encourages to write Jewish. Naomi from the Young Eagles Club encourages me to write English. I don't think I will ever be a poetess. I haven't enough… I'd rather be a nurse. I only write because I don't want my imagination "to rush away with one," that is when I get a pretty idea, I set it down so that I shouldn't forget it.

My first poem that I wrote was published in the "Eagle" on the 9th January, 1921. It is called "The Fair Sad Maid." Many other pieces have I written. I want to keep them as a remembrance of my childhood when I grow up.

Shulamis recorded many aspects of her life in dozens of private
notebooks, beginning in 1927.
Jewish Public Library.

ॐ Diary entry April 30, 1927

I have been told by many that I have talent for the stage (I recite in
plays for the Peretz School), but I would rather stick to my mode of
living, becoming a nurse, helping the needy, writing the ideas. I am
still a child, but who knows what time has in store for me.
Sophie Borodensky, April 30, 1927

ॐ Diary entry May 9, 1992 [age seventy-nine]

Ann Scofield – Transformative workshop
It reminds me of my own trauma which reminds me of Aaron's
death, – my birth father killed in CPR accident while connecting
wires on a roof top. When the policeman brings the news to Mamma,
there is panic, horror –
I, not quite 5 months old.

I seem (over the years) to absolutely recall the sequence:

 - police at door

 - Mamma's hysterical response

 - My Bubbie's house where everyone is in panic

 - I, the infant on the table, screaming for attention while everyone is busy with Mamma – Bubbie in control – Bubbie who mourned him, her eldest, 29 yrs, all the days of her life, never permitted herself any pleasure, because she believed his death was meant as a punishment to her because she was "a sinful woman."

 - Distant and unbelievable as it may seem, I truly believe that that was the moment when I became the outsider & have remained so ever since in my heart.

∾ Diary entry November 22, 1933 [age twenty]

Happiness is a thing to end a fairy tale with. There is no such thing, natural or synthetic. Monotony, dull monotony, and still eating pain. There is no room, no time for a dream.

So, after all, my life is to be a dull streak, – ambition, desire, to be suppressed, varying only by a sudden outburst of inner pain and anger at all about me and in the end, not even that, just a dull inanimate existence? God, let me die, rather than live to a ripe old age on such an existence!

I can't fathom it. I can't realize it all. It seems like a black shroud thrown over me, that will soon be lifted and again expose the light. It has all come as suddenly, so awfully suddenly!

∾ Diary entry January 11, 1934 [age twenty]

This is the first time in, oh, ever so long that this has happened to me. I have been through the uttermost depths of hell, since I last wrote; through the gloom so black I thought I could never see any light.

Shulamis often decorated her diaries. This one included her
Yiddish poetry, "Leeder" (Poetry), as the title indicates.
Jewish Public Library.

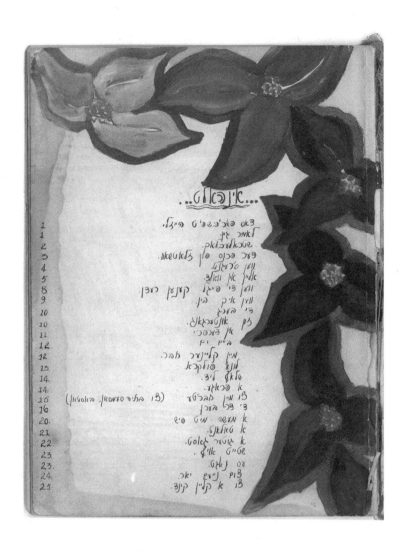

The Contents page of her diary containing Yiddish poetry.
Jewish Public Library.

But somehow, today the horrible shroud seemed to lift itself & once more I feel the force of laughter bubbling in me! I could let out a long halloooo & a shriek!

There is a feeling of spring in the air. Everything is thawy & oozy, there is no sun, but a sort of delicious feeling of warmth.

On my way from school I caught it in myself. I snatched my hat from my head and let the soft air glide quickly and lightly through my unbrushed hair. I felt my head rise higher & and stand quite erect on my usually, of late, drooping shoulders. I jumped onto a mound of snow on the side of the sidewalk & was just ready to scream out, "I'm the king of the castle, I'm the king of the castle", when I suddenly realized, after all I am big...

I spoke to my dentist about "Moon and Sixpence" & "Of Human Bondage" and I felt the old thrill come through me again as when I first read them, and I saw before me Cranshaw's [Miss Cranshaw, her former fourth grade teacher at Strathearn School] answer to the riddle of life: the carpet with its intricate pattern of life...colorful, - the colors of pain & misery, liberating, suddenly, in certain tiny spaces, the quietly glowing color of joy & happiness!

Oh, how good, how full & vivid & alive! Only after experiencing deep misery can one really feel glad! Glad about nothing, – just glad. It is stronger, more propelling than mind, that certain peculiar feeling of gladness that gets one and seems to caress the heart for no good reason at all – just gladness and a desire to laugh!

◌ Diary entry February 6, 1984

I find it difficult to reread what I've written. No patience? Fear of what I'll find? And yet, those diaries, those short rememberings are the seeds for new stories. I'm glad I wrote them.

Perhaps this is my first real self-recognition as a writer.

∾ Diary entry March 27, 1986

I should be spending the time I use for this diary in creative writing. I never read this stuff back. I just seem to need to do this to convince myself I'm alive.

∾ Diary entry February 15, 1987

Well, seems I've given up writing altogether – even in this journal. I used to write early and now I haven't even bothered to do that. I guess that's one way to get rid of the conflict & guilt of not writing – just to "throw out the baby with the bathwater" no creative (prose or poetry) work? Nothing at all.
While the days have been equally full, I've just not recorded anything. A pity. But at least I've not been eating myself up about it.

∾ Diary entry March 5, 1987

I've written so little all winter, I've lost the knack. I want to restore the desire to write.

∾ Diary entry August 1, 1991

My diary, my catharsis. I don't phone people, learned long ago to keep most people at a distance. The less they know about me, the better. <u>I'm the great success. Keep out!</u>

Roots: Grandparents and Parents

Vichna Dobkin was involved from an early age in the socialist movement in Chernobyl (Russia at that time, now Ukraine). The only daughter and youngest of five surviving children, at the age of twenty she left her family and friends behind and came to Canada in 1910, along with her husband Aaron Borodensky, shortly after their marriage in Chernobyl. Her mother and two brothers remained in Chernobyl and two of her brothers settled in New York City.

Aaron Borodensky was one of thirteen children and an idealistic, charismatic leader of the socialist movement in Chernobyl. The whole Borodensky family, including Aaron's parents, his wife Vichna, and his siblings, left their home and came to Canada to escape the incessant pogroms and to find a better life. They settled in Montreal. Aaron and Vichna's only child Sophie (later Shulamis) was born in Montreal on April 12, 1913.

Aaron was tragically killed in a work accident at the age of twenty-nine on August 24, 1913 when Shulamis was just a few months old. Vichna and her baby daughter continued to live with Aaron's family; on May 2, 1916 Vichna married Aaron's younger brother Philip (nineteen years old at the time) and they rented a flat nearby. Vichna and Philip had two children together: Dena (May 27, 1917–December 4, 1958) and Pesach Aarel, called Arele. Dena, called Deenie, later became Deenie Aronovitch. Arele died before his third birthday.

Philip Borodensky was apprenticed to a tailor at the age of five in Chernobyl and, after migrating to Canada with the large Borodensky family, became an expert and much sought-after custom tailor of men's suits. In Montreal he established *Broadway Tailors*, a custom tailor shop, first located on The Main (Saint Lawrence Street, now Saint-Laurent Boulevard) and then on Peel, near Sherbrooke Street. After many years he closed the shop, but – semi-retired and assisted by Vichna – he continued to do his fine tailoring from their apartment on Decarie Boulevard, near Queen Mary.

To Shulamis and Deenie, Philip was a devoted father – their beloved "Papa" – and despite the fact that he was seven years her junior, he was also a dedicated husband to Vichna. Vichna was chronically ill, often bedridden, and sometimes hospitalized in a tuberculosis sanatorium in Sainte-Agathe-des-Monts, in the Laurentian Mountains, until a simple operation in 1944 repaired the bronchial condition from which she had suffered, misdiagnosed, for more than thirty years. Because of their mother's chronic illness, Shulamis and Deenie spent much of their childhood living with their paternal grandparents, their cherished Bubbie and Zaida, since Philip was unable to properly care for them while carrying on the tailoring business that provided their only income.

∾ Diary entry December 16, 1971

To have been the spoiled darling the 7th & only one to survive – an *ogbange* (the spoiled child) – to have been sold to the lady next door so the evil spirits will have no access to her, to have married a "father figure" – a man who worshipped her, Aaron was the leader of the Socialist Movement in the shtetl and the man who brought her to the table and served her breakfast & put her back to bed – (she was delicate 4 months out of childbed with me) – & then to be mid-morn informed that he'd been cut in half with a passing saw while he was connecting wires on a rooftop – to have remarried – to a man with whom she really couldn't have been in love – he was only a 19 yr. old kid – have 2 children with him – Dena & Aarele (who died at 2½ Denie at 41), to have spent most of her life in bed & in Sans; spitting up blood yet not having TB – this vivacious high-spirited very intelligent woman – with so much dignity, content with every small pleasure with a capacity for enjoyment & laughter & dancing – & to the last of her 80 yrs of wholeness always dressed prettily, youthfully, carrying responsibility in the Peretz Shule on Bd. Of Directors & the Froyen Farein Treasurer all those years & slender & straight, on neat shoes with her spanking white gloves, always – a personality – a little over-exuberant sometimes, like myself – but logical & bright & energetic – always *balebatish* (respectable home-owner), never in debt – always with dignity – with the capacity for appreciation & enjoyment far beyond her education and her many years –

(Top) Shulamis' mother's friends in Chernobyl.
(Bottom) A tailor shop in Chernobyl.
Jewish Public Library.

Aaron is seated at right. Person on left, and year of photo are unknown.
Jewish Public Library.

A KOPEK FOR MAMA

FOR YEARS I HAD HEARD Mamma's *Chernobyler landsman* (a fellow immigrant from one's native home, in this case, Chernobyl), Benyamin, call Mamma *shvesterl* (little sister). It seemed strange that he should do so, but I didn't like to ask. He called her *shvesterl* out of fondness, I thought, because he was so much older than her, and because he was a loving, affectionate *landsman*.

As a matter of fact, all her *landsmen* thought the world of Mamma. She was known as *Vichna die Roita*, Vichna the Redhead. Her abundant auburn hair signalled her outgoing personality, and she liked to tell how, as a youngster in Chernobyl, clinging to her mother's apron on the way to market, she would throw a tantrum because the boys chased her shouting, "Pozshar!" ("Fire!")

Mamma's photograph, taken shortly after her arrival in the Golden Land, shows her as a tall, attractive young woman with a shy smile, a full bosom, her hair piled high in soft puffs. She wears a black ankle-length taffeta gown pinched in at the waist, a fine lace inset fitting into the deeply cut square neck, and a velvet band around her throat. A gold pince-nez with black ribbon attempts to camouflage the fact that her left eye is turned in, the result of a severe fright in early childhood. Lips open, she looks eager and expectant.

Mamma was constantly ailing and rarely entertained, but she was fond of people: vivacious among women, flirtatious with men. Her *landsmen* always compared her to her mother, my grandmother, Chassia Dobkin, whom they had known "at home."

I liked to hear Mamma tell of "home." "We came from a well-to-do family, a family of *yichus* (status) in Chernobyl," Mamma reminisced. "My father, Shloime Dobkin, had been a master tailor with his own house and his own shop. After his death my mother took over the shop. *Chassia die Kluga*, Chassia the Wise, they called her." Mamma smiled with pleasant memory. "People liked to work for Chassia Dobkin because she fed them well."

"You know how Chassia tested a workman?" she wistfully recalled. "She offered him a meal and sat with him while he ate. If he eats quickly and neatly, he'll work quickly and well, she reasoned."

Mamma was the youngest of the Dobkin family, with four older brothers. Mamma was the last of seven daughters born to Chassia and Shloime Dobkin; the other girls had died in infancy.

When a seventh daughter was born to them, Chassia and Shloime decided something must be done to outwit the demons. The rabbi suggested that another name be added to her given name, Vichna (she had been named for a maternal grandmother). The name Chaya, which means "life," or Alta, "the aged one," could be added, both emphasizing that she was to live to a ripe old age. Either one of these could block the power of the evil Lilith, who sucked away mother's milk and killed newborn children.

But the women in the *shtetl* suggested an even more drastic measure – one rarely used, but valid under the circumstances. The thing to do was to "sell" the infant to one's next-door neighbour so the demon would be confused and thus lose her prey. "She's no longer the daughter of Shloime and Chassia," they reasoned, "now she belongs to Chaim and Channah." So the ceremony was set up.

Chaim and Channah came to visit the new mother and Chassia offered to sell them her new daughter.

"How much do you want for her?"

"Ten kopeks."

"Ten kopeks? Ridiculous! Ten kopeks for a girl? And a redhead at that! You must be out of your heads! We'll give you one kopek." (This was to show the demon what a worthless article this was.)

"One kopek? Listen to her! One can see she spilt no blood over her! Make it seven."

"Seven kopeks? Mad! The woman must be mad. Just look at that long, skinny, yowling brat! One kopek – and not a hair more. Take it or leave it!"

"But – "

"No buts. Come, Chaim – " and Channah turned to go.

"All right! All right! Don't be so hasty!" *Chassia die Kluga* called them back. "Take her for a kopek. But look after her well . . ."

"Done," said Channah. "Khaim, give her the kopek."

Then, turning to her husband and shaking her head in the direction of Chassia's bed: "And if she thinks she's being cheated, we'll let *her* bring the girl up. But, remember, Chassia, the girl is *ours*. She's not yours any more. She will call me *Mamma* and Chaim

Tata. And our children will be her brothers and sister. Remember –
and don't forget!"

And so the deal was made and the kopek changed hands. And as
Moses, foundling of the Pharaoh's daughter, was brought up by
Jokheved, his true mother, so Vichna, purchased by Chaim and
Channah, was brought up by her own mother, calling both Channah
and Chassia "Mamma," and being called *shvesterl* by the children of
both families. And indeed, she grew as beloved and pampered as
any princess could be.

And that was why Benyamin, her one-time neighbour and ever-
loving *landsman*, called Mamma *shvesterl*.

∼

MAMMA LEAVES FOR THE GOLDEN LAND

MAMMA LIKED TO TELL US how she came to Canada as a new bride.
Again and again she told us how she left her mother to come to
Canada, the Golden Land.

Mamma liked to remind us that she had crossed the Atlantic
twice. The first time she came alone to visit her two brothers "in
America," New York to be precise, and the second time she came to
settle in Montreal with her young husband, the socialist dreamer.
In Montreal there was already a small contingent of *Chernobyler
Landsleit*, among them two of Papa's brothers and Mamma's
"brother," her neighbour Benyamin. They wrote home of available
work on the Canadian Pacific Railway (CPR) and in the various
needle trades, inviting others to join them.

By 1910 the situation in Russia had long signalled the need to
leave *Fonya's Medina*, "Fonya" being the nickname for the Czar.

"Which Jew wanted to serve the Russian Czar?" Mamma would
ask rhetorically. "What was there to be thankful for? Jews couldn't
live in a big city. We couldn't study at the university unless we
converted, and many still remembered living through those terrible
pogroms… And as young socialists, we were in constant danger of

arrest and being sent on the 'Y trap' – to go on foot to Siberia… Is it any wonder everyone began to look to the Golden Land?"

"But it was very hard for me to leave my mother," Mamma added sadly.

"Ask her to come with us," her bridegroom had urged. But Chassia Dobkin had refused. Her two eldest sons were unwilling to uproot themselves and their families, and Chassia had decided to remain with her sons, and in her own house.

"Here everyone knows me," she said. "Here I am Chassia Dobkin. And there? Who knows how much longer the good Lord will spare me? I'll stay." Deep within, of course, she hoped her daughter and her son-in-law would, in time, return to Chernobyl.

As the wedding drew nearer, Chassia Dobkin grew silent. She went about her usual daily rounds but her sighs and momentary lapses of memory belied her composure.

"Tfoo!" she would say, "Where did I put the meat knife! I just had it in my hand! There are *shedim* (ghosts) in the house lately! I can't find a thing I put down!"

Her daughter heard her with a heavy heart. "Mamma," she tried again, "Why don't you come with us? You have two sons here but you also have two sons in America!"

"So?" said Chassia, "I'll be a mother-in-law in a son-in-law's house? My husband lies buried in the Old Cemetery. All my graves are here," she added with a flash from her brimming eyes. "Me, *Fonya* doesn't want for his army. Go with your husband. A wife's place is with her husband. If God wills it, we will meet again. May good fortune come to greet you."

The wedding festivities were dampened by the impending parting. The fine trousseau with its handmade lace and embroideries had been prepared some months earlier, and it lay packed in steamer trunks. Soon after the wedding, the horse-drawn wagon rolled up to the door to pick up the baggage and bring it to the ferry that would be leaving for Kiev. There the newlyweds would board the steamer for America.

It was not a happy scene. Few words were spoken as relatives and friends embraced the pair, filling the last moments with the usual small talk to cover up the pain of parting.

"Don't forget to write!" "Don't forget to write often!" various voices called. "Give regards to Benyamin and the *Landsleit!*" "Go in good health and don't forget to write *full postcards!*" cried Khaim and Channah.

Mamma's brothers kissed her fondly again. Noyach, the eldest, said, "Go in good health, little sister. Travel under a lucky star. Write often and remember – this is always your home…"

As they gathered at the wharf, Chassia Dobkin stood still like a stone figure. No word, no tear. Her sons and friends pressed forward to embrace and kiss her Vichnele goodbye. Chassia stood at her daughter's side, her long skirt riveted to the grass, her hands clasped under her clean white apron. The ends of her silk kerchief quivered beneath her chin as, with eyes shut, she seemed to be muttering some unheard prayer. As her daughter turned to embrace her, she let out a low moan. Suddenly she was sobbing loudly, crying brokenly. The young husband looked to his bride's brothers. The ferry was ready to depart. Noyach put his hands on his mother's shoulders and, firmly but gently, tore her from her daughter's embrace. A loud cry broke from the mother's being as her daughter turned away, her head pressed against her husband's sleeve. As the ferry left the dock, Chassia let out a long, loud wail, "Vichnele Vichnele my child, my heart tells me I'll never see you again!"

Vichna Dobkin, with her beloved Aaron Borodensky, were on their way to the New World, Canada – part of the Golden *Medina.*

~

RITES OF PASSAGE

My Bubbie's attitudes towards life and death were straight-forward.

"First comes life, then comes death. God gives and God takes away. Some live long, some are not long for this world. In between, so long as one lives, one must try to be a *mentch.*"

"What's a *mentch*, Bubbie?" I asked, sitting beside her as she peeled potatoes in her basement kitchen.

(Top) Some of the Borodensky children with Vichna and Aaron front row;
Philip in middle, back row.
(Bottom) Bubby and Zaida with Shulamis, circa 1913.
Jewish Public Library.

"A *mentsch* knows he was put here to follow the Commandments. A *mentsch* thinks of others and tries to help those who need him. He also knows he shouldn't do to someone what he doesn't like for himself. A *mentch* remembers: after this world comes the Real World, the *Olam ha-Emess*, and we have to answer for our time here. All you can leave of yourself here is a good name."

Until the time of her death, my Bubbie carried herself straight and tall. "*Tselem Elohim*," she repeated, tapping me on the back to straighten up. "In His image He made us. A person has to walk straight and tall no one should have to pity him. He should live as well as he can but not tear out anyone's eyes with envy. He should always remember to look down – so many people have less…"

No one knew the exact date of Bubbie's birth. Nor did her children know their own birthdates. All had been inscribed in the synagogue registry in Chernobyl according to the Jewish lunar calendar. Birthdays were associated with events: for example, six weeks after the fire in the marketplace; a month before Chaim Ber left for America; or with holidays: three days before Succoth, two weeks after Chanukah. My own birthday on April 12 was remembered as eight days before Passover. When birthdates became mandatory for school in Canada, the children chose approximated dates. In this way, Bubbie's birthday was set for Purim, the Feast of Esther.

Purim. The very name evokes memories. How many Purims had we celebrated in my Bubbie's house? How many marches with my Zaida to the Shomrim Laboker Synagogue to hear the reading of the *Megillah*, the Book of Esther, proudly carrying our noise-makers, our *graggers*, which we would whirl to blot out the name of the evil Haman? Then the return to Bubbie's house for the Purim feast, to the house which rang with the voices of family and friends, the house exulting with the aroma of peppercorns, poppy seed, and honey – symbols of survival, fruitfulness, and a sweet life.

I, who had grown up in a secular world, envied Bubbie her gifts of piety and faith.

"One must always remember God's goodness," she said. "God has been good to me. Of the thirteen children He gave me, not counting the miscarriages, I raised ten. So many women lost most of their brood in childbed, not of us be it said… But as the Rabbi says, 'For the very young one must not mourn. Who knows what they might have grown up to be?'

"But why did He take my firstborn when he was already a man? Such a good man – such a good son…" She paused a moment, sighed, then continued stoically, "One mustn't question. No doubt I was a sinful woman…"

I could not imagine what sins this good woman might have committed. Yet until the end of her days my Bubbie did penance, fasting on Mondays and Thursdays and allowing herself no pleasure than those related to her family, her synagogue, or a neighbour's needs.

After her seventieth birthday, Bubbie said, "Now every day is a gift. All we are promised is threescore and ten." And she applied herself even more fervently to the service of those less fortunate, dropping more coins into the various alms boxes for the needy she would never see, feeding her "regulars," the poor who came for a meal on given days before the family returned from work, and to the animals who found shelter by her stove. "God's creatures," she would say. "And what are we here for?"

By her eightieth birthday, Bubbie had grown very frail. Her soft face had grown thin and wan; her gentle mouth had shrunk to a pale faint line over her toothless gums. Yet she insisted on maintaining her Monday and Thursday fasts. To her children's remonstrations and rebukes, she always had the same response: "Why? Why should I change now? God has been good to me. I'll live as long as he wants me to live – not a day less, not a day more. The worms will have enough to eat as it is."

When the Purim of her eighty-second birthday came around, my Bubbie said, "Who knows what tomorrow will bring?" And she decided to make a party.

This was another Purim. It was not in the big old house on Cadieux and Pine, the house of memory. It was in a downstairs flat on Esplanade Avenue, facing the playing fields of Mount Royal, within walking distance of the synagogue Bubbie attended when she felt strong enough to walk.

It was a long time since the family had assembled. Surrounded by her sons and daughters and their married and unmarried children,

Bubbie looked radiant despite her frailty. She wore her freshly dressed peruke and her black Sabbath dress.

The table was heavy with the remembered delicacies Bubbie had made. My eye passed from the crackling Russian strudels, brown and fragrant, packed with raisins, cinnamon, nuts, and homemade jams, to the wispy noodle kugels leafed with apples, to the gefilte fish, white with specks of black pepper and bits of bright carrot.

"Bubbie, when did you do all this?" I asked.

"I wake so early. I can't stay in bed – so I cooked. Come help me bring in the Purim *gebeks*."

My Bubbie's Purim *gebeks*: the beloved *hamantashen* (Haman's pockets, named for Haman's triangular hat), stuffed with poppy seed and honey; the *taiglach*, those mounds of flaky pastry morsels lightly baked, clustered with walnuts in boiling buckwheat honey; the honey-laced sesame-seed squares sprinkled with ginger, flaunting their allspice like incense… As I helped her carry in the platters, all my childhood images of Queen Esther's feasts rose before me. When she brought in the enormous plaited ceremonial loaf, the Purim *koilitch*, and set it before the five-branched silver candelabrum, it seemed to me for a moment that the clock had been turned back to the years of my childhood again, only Zaida was no longer there to preside over this Purim feast.

Everyone brought birthday presents. When I had asked my Bubbie what she would like, she said, "I have everything I need. If you would like to give me some money, I'll give it to the synagogue. They'll know what to do with it."

I kissed Bubbie, and in Yiddish, wished her a happy birthday: "May you have many good years before you, Bubbie darling."

"Thank you *Donyela*," she nodded wistfully. "Every day is God-granted. I only pray when the time comes He will give me a little time to prepare myself and won't let me suffer too long."

Suddenly there was a sense of separation in the air. I could not imagine there would ever be a time without Bubbie.

I looked at Papa and Mamma, at the aunties and uncles seated around the dining room. They were aging. Where were the bouncing voices of former years? I walked into the living room where the cousins and thirty-two grandchildren, who spoke only English, were chatting politely, impersonally. The kinship which had once held the family together had become a thin filament that bound them only at bar mitzvahs, weddings, and funerals. I recalled the time Papa had wanted to move our family to California because of Mamma's health and Bubbie had cried, "What? Break up the family? What else have I got?" And we had stayed. I recalled a holiday afternoon visit with Papa at Bubbie's house.

"Nobody hardly comes," she mourned.

"Everyone is busy with his own life," Papa tried to comfort her.

"It's the telephone to blame. The telephone broke up the family," she insisted. "Before, we all lived near each other – upstairs, downstairs, around the corner, next block. In two minutes we were by each other. Now a quick ring: 'Hello Mamma.' 'Hello *Shviger*.' Finished. I sit alone." I knew Papa was uncomfortable. If only he could smoke, but he would not defile the day in his mother's presence.

"What can you do? It's America," he condoned. "It's America not Chernobyl. It's different times…"

I returned to the dining room. Tea was served. The platters grew empty. People got ready to leave.

"Wait," said Bubbie. "There's a lot left. Take some home for tomorrow."

"Nothing has really changed," I tried to comfort myself. "May we all celebrate your birthday again next year, Bubbie darling," I offered as I kissed her good night.

"His will be done," she said returning my embrace. I took my package of strudel and *hamantashen* and went into the quiet street.

Two weeks later, Bubbie tripped in her kitchen and broke a hip. The doctor said nothing could be done for her; she must just rest in bed.

When I came to see her she was dozing. I sat by her bed in the twilit room and waited for her to open her eyes.

"How are you feeling, Bubbie?"

"*Donyela*, no one lives forever. I only ask I shouldn't be a burden for long. We have a good God in heaven…"

Bubbie lingered for two weeks weaving in and out of consciousness. The doctor came daily. The children came and went. She died in her own house, in her own bed.

The one piece of clothing of which my Bubbie was proud was her shroud. Periodically, when the family was assembled, she would take it out and show it off. "See how well it is made?" she would finger it appreciatively. "Broad and long, too. So the feet will be covered properly. Not like by poor old Mrs. Reisman, may her soul rest in peace. A shame! A shame! Such a short shroud! Everyone could see the tips of her feet!" Then, turning to her own again, "See the nice stitches? The women took care to make it nice." She was referring to the ladies of the Burial Society of the Shomrim Laboker Synagogue, the new *shul* on Saint Dominique St. near Prince Arthur, where my Zaida, the carpenter, had a special place of honour, since he, with his own hands, had helped build it.

The older sons and daughters smiled with restraint, but the younger members of the family responded with annoyance and distaste.

"Mamma, for Heaven's sake, put that thing away! It's terrible! Who wants to think of such things now? And in the middle of a pleasant afternoon yet, when the children are here!"

But Bubbie was adamant, nonplussed. "Why the fuss? A person has to be ready at all times. When the Angel of Death calls, you can't be a pig and refuse. You have to go. After all, this life is just a station on the road to the Real World. A person has to be prepared."

On several occasions different shrouds were brought out and offered for inspection. "I had to give my other one away. Poor Mrs. Frumkin died on the eve of the Sabbath, unprepared! The beadle came over. She was my size (not of me be it said). So the women made me this one. I told you a person has to be prepared..."

I don't recall the Rabbi's words. I only recall the crowded funeral parlour on St. Urbain Street and the ten tall sons and daughters standing to have the razor blade cut into the black cloth of their clothing, the cut of *Kriah*, of separation from the dead, and I recall the long cortège following the hearse. Most clearly I recall the strangers, old people who pushed their way through the crowd to touch the hearse, to ask the traditional forgiveness and to beg her intercession for them in the *Olam Habah*, the World to Come.

"Intercede for me, Chaya Raizl, intercede for me!" pleaded an old crone. "You were a *mentch*, a *Tsnuah*, a modest Jewish soul," she continued, keeping her hand on the slowly moving hearse, "an honest Jewish daughter…"

"Where will we eat on Wednesdays?" wailed an old beggar. "May your goodness come to greet you. You were a *mentch*."

A grey wind drove the leaves across the open yard of Mount Royal School on St. Urbain Street where I had attended kindergarten. Facing it, across the way, stood the synagogue where Bubbie had worshipped. As the cortège stopped for a respectful moment, I stood bonded by an ancient rite.

"Bubbie darling, intercede for me," I, the agnostic granddaughter, wept into my handkerchief. "Intercede for me, for my family, for us all…"

Bubbie darling, with your passing my childhood was gone forever.

Bordensky family late 1930s celebrate Bubby and Zaida's 50th Wedding Anniversary, Montreal.
Jewish Public Library.

A Montreal Childhood

Preface to the 1983 edition of *Shulamis: Stories from a Montreal Childhood.*

I N 1963, WHEN THE JEWISH PERETZ SCHOOL celebrated its fiftieth anniversary, a strange yearning awoke in me to return to the old street in that one-time Jewish neighbourhood. It was at least twenty years since I had last visited the area.

The Peretz School, the *Shule*, is a vivid part of my childhood memory: not the bright new one on Cote-St-Luc with its broad halls and floors and neon-lighted days; not the many rented flats where children spent the dimly lit after-school hours seeking to tie the elusive knots which bound them to their ancient, many-storied past; not even the renovated building (formerly a factory) on Duluth Street where I taught the first day-school kindergarten, which had opened its doors gratis to children of survivors of the Holocaust.

My *Shule* was in the great old house on Cadieux Street (now de Bullion) above Prince Arthur, across from the iron-fenced stone nunnery with its tall trees and mystery-shrouded dormer windows, a hundred or more yards from the Jewish Maternity Hospital from which weird wailings could be heard in my Bubbie's house next door. Flanked by the red brick walls of neighbouring houses, the school stood in modest retirement off the busy street. Its large bay windows, like heavy-lidded eyes, bore witness to the changing tempo, changing times. Its grey slotted box-benches concealed untold childhood treasures: a well-sharpened pencil, slipped from the hands of a child completing his homework or resting from his games; a large copper penny with a portrait of King George; a tiny silver five-cent piece – today a collector's item. The large earthen courtyard harboured a long elm with patches of grass trying valiantly to grow around it despite the constant traffic of children's feet. The well-worn winding stairs within were alive, singing their many-voiced descants to the psalms of our youthful ascents and descents.

That was a long time ago.

The sun is bright and a premature spring wind ruffles the puddles that steal their way into the gaps in the snow. I hail a cab and ask to be released at the corner of the street where I had lived.

As I walk up Coloniale Avenue I seem to feel a previous incarnation. The house we lived in, with its winding iron staircase, still stands. It looks loved and cared for with its coat of fresh paint and cheerful curtains. On these stairs I had skidded on a cold winter's day when, in fantasy of being a beautiful famous actress, I had let go of the banister and had hit bottom on my dignity. Here, on the other side of the lane where we had skipped and played marbles, stands the old Malo house where, after Mr. Malo's death, little bleeding hearts had blown in the tiny garden every summer. Now the outer wooden doors had been removed.

On all sides memories jostle each other as I look about, recalling moments, people, and dreams. The only false note comes from the newfangled street lamp, which replaces the one I recalled, the one that stood right across from our parlour window, casting in the night an intricate pattern through the lace curtains of our triptych bay window onto the carpeted floor.

I mustn't stop. There, across the road is the high wooden fence with the latched door through which I used to find my way up the back stairs into the school on Cadieux Street. Yet, as I look, the building seems to have vanished. The fence is there but I find no sign of the building above it.

I move quickly down Prince Arthur Street. It is quite as it was. The names on the shops are different but the buildings are the same. On the left is Choquette's Candy Store, still a candy store, but no longer owned by the angry, moustached little Frenchman who hated children yet sold only candy and tobacco. Beside it is the Chinese laundry. Is this the laundryman who gave me lychee nuts when I came for our package and a glorious many-coloured glass bangle at Christmas?

Our neighbour, Malo's stately candy shop, still stands diagonally opposite Dover's Grocery, but here the decorous wooden doors have been removed and a shabby glass business window announces some textile firm.

Quickly I hurry up the street. How many times had I hurried up this same street in fear of being late, in fear of missing something at the *Shule*?

Yet I seem to be taking too many steps. Between the two tall red brick walls that seem to have grown so strangely close together, the courtyard where we played has become a brown muddy square, deeply gouged with the massive tires of freight trucks. Three men are loading merchandise into a truck. But where is the *Shule*? There in the background beyond the walls, stands an old brown longhouse.

Surely there is some mistake. I probably hadn't gone far enough up the street. I must look a little further.

But no, I recognize my Bubbie's house and, beside it, the large glass-windowed doors with the *Mogen Davids*, the windows of the sadly neglected Jewish Maternity Hospital. It is now a private dwelling with several shabby-looking children sitting on the steps.

How it had all changed since my early remembering! Gone are the long slotted benches upon which we had sat. There's not even a vestige of the chalk marks of our childhood on the recently repainted red brick walls. The *Shule*, like a shrunken aging giant, stared sombrely at me across the empty courtyard.

There is a sense of loss in me – a sense of bereavement.

I look with suspended breath across the street for that other landmark, the nunnery with its beautiful garden. The grey building stands denuded, stripped of its trees and bushes – it is now a factory. The "dismounting stone" in front of its gate is gone; in an earlier day gracious ladies had used it to step from their horse-drawn carriages to the sidewalk.

An era has passed away.

EARLY SORROW

IT WAS IN THE DOWNSTAIRS flat on Coloniale Avenue above Rachel that I first knew the pain of separation. Out of its large, glass, front-parlour window, I could see the tall tree with its sparsely leafed branches of early spring, but I recall no sunshine in that room. I recall only a grey morning mist through which a little girl of three, with blond bottle curls, always properly dressed, moved silently, holding a large round silver balloon on a stick, marching round and round in a parade of her own.

That was the spring we moved out of my Bubbie's house to a place of our own.

Suddenly it was quiet. No longer was there the chorus of voices of the young aunts and uncles returning from work or school; no longer was there the bustle of my Bubbie's quick-moving long white apron or the rattle of the large pots and pans on the wood stove in the basement kitchen as she prepared the meals and baked the bread for the large, busy family. We were alone in our own flat, Papa, Mamma, and I: Mamma in the kitchen, Papa at work, and I – at the large window looking out. I played with the towel-dolls my Mamma made for me: faceless dolls, ephemeral playmates made by bunching one end of the towel into a head and wrapping the rest around it. How I had hugged and cuddled and tended them in their shoebox carriages, which I pulled about with an attached string!

At night we were together in the back parlour that served as the family bedroom: Papa and Mamma in the big bed in the middle of the room, I in my small bed in the corner to the right.

I felt even lonelier at night.

"Why can't I sleep with you and Papa?" I begged.

"You're a big girl now," said Mamma. "You're three years old. We have our own house and you have your own bed because you are a big girl."

I did not feel very big. I felt very lonely. I missed the large family of aunts and uncles who scolded and fussed over me. I missed the embracing warmth of that big house.

The only one I did not miss was the auntie Faygel. She was dark and squat and always dressed in black. Her eyes were eternally angry

Philip, Vichna, and Sophie (Shulamis), circa 1916.
Photo by L. Baum. Jewish Public Library.

and she never opened her mouth without issuing what I heard as a snarl. Even her laughter was a yelp. She was childless and liked to pinch me with the stubby fingers of her short, stout hand. I was afraid of her and ran to hide behind Mamma whenever she was there.

On Saturday nights, when the family gathered around my Bubbie's great dining room table, Auntie Faygel refused to sit down. She stood behind my Zaida's chair under the big wooden clock with the brown horse ornament. She neither spoke nor ate: the skeleton at the feast.

In the new house, she began to appear to me in a recurring nightmare.

I awoke screaming, "Mamma! Mamma!"

In the dream she was standing in her accustomed place behind Zaida's chair under the clock. The family was enjoying the feast Bubbie had set before them, but she was not part of the celebration. She was glowering at me, as would the clock. Suddenly she pointed at me with her yellow fingernail.

"Mamma!"

"She's dreaming," said Papa, turning on the light.

He picked me up and sat me on his lap at the edge of their bed.

"It's Auntie Faygel!" I sobbed shrilly, clinging to him in terror. "With the horse."

"It's only a dream," said Papa, rocking me gently. "Only a dream. What is the Auntie doing?"

"She's winding up the big clock in Bubbie's dining room! And the clock is screaming and the horsey is jumping on me!"

I trembled as I related the horror of my nightmare.

"It's nothing!" Mamma comforted, coming close to us. "See? Nobody is here, just Papa and you and me…"

"You had a bad dream," Papa repeated. "That horsey on the clock is a toy horse. He can't hurt you…"

"But Auntie Faygel!" I cried.

"She isn't even here. See? It's just a bad dream," Mamma repeated.

"Wait, I'll get you a glass of water so it'll go away," Papa offered, returning me to my own bed.

The nightmare recurred again and again and in my own small bed I felt lonelier than ever.

One Sunday morning, Mamma dressed me early in a white silky dress she had sewn for me, a dress which I clearly recall had little pink flowers scattered over it, a dress with a small frill at the hem and neckline. As she combed my hair into curls and tied them to one side with a pink ribbon, she said, "Today we are going to Dominion Park. We will have lots of fun there."

It was a long ride by tram to the amusement park. Papa carried me on and off the car in his arms and, out of the distant past, I recall my first sight of that magical country with its huge Ferris wheel, its little red flags moving round and round, its metal baskets cradling its squealing passengers high above the crowd.

A greater wonder was soon to appear before me. I dragged Papa to where the music was pulling me, the music of the calliope that played for the galloping ponies of the merry-go-round.

What beautiful ponies! Painted ponies with trappings in crimson, silver, and gold! I must ride one of them – that white one with the crimson bridle and the golden mane!

As we waited for the ride to come to an end, Papa bought me a silver balloon and soon I was ensconced on the white wooden pony of my choice, clinging to his golden mane, terrified yet elated. The music started up again and we were away. Up and down and round and round to the music of the calliope we went, on an unreal pony to the real world of childhood. The screams that were first heard as the music started again subsided with our rising joy.

It was hard to pry me off that pony. It was only the bribe of that silver balloon that got me off.

I was up early the next morning, eyeing my silver balloon as it stood bobbing gently, tied to the corner of my bed on its tall, thin stick. How I had prized and fondled it until bedtime! It was the symbol of all my pleasure of the day at the fair, the day that for a time had wiped out that loneliness which had enwrapped me.

I don't recall what I wore that morning. I recall myself only in that silky dress, the little girl with the blond curls and sad face, holding my balloon upright in my left hand, marching round and round in the front parlour under the high ceiling, humming my own little tune in imitation of the calliope, riding my imaginary gold-maned pony, watching my reflection in the tall floor mirror that stood in the corner by the window.

Mamma looked in for a moment, smiled, and walked away.

The room was warm and I continued on my imaginary ride, along with the remembered troupe of ponies, following my lead, the sound of the calliope echoing in my ears.

Suddenly there was a loud bang. I shrieked. Mamma came running. I was crying wildly.

My balloon had burst in the warm air near the ceiling. It hung in silver tatters.

ENTER DEENIE — THE NEW BABY

Soon Mamma began to spend her mornings in bed. Papa served me my breakfast and I played quietly in the front parlour while Mamma spent the morning in bed. Later she would rise to fix our lunch and then Mamma and I would go for a short walk. Often we stopped at the shop windows to admire their wares.

As time wore on, Mamma began to stop at The Main Furniture Store. "See that nice baby carriage?" she would ask. "Like for a doll but bigger. For a real baby." I nodded my approval and we walked on.

I was glad to be spending so much time with Mamma. I was beginning to accept the new house and the condition of aloneness in the family. Over and over again Mamma told me I was a Big Girl, not a baby like my auntie's baby who still suckled at the breast. I could feed myself and could even dress myself, except for tying the laces of my tall shoes. I could play by myself for hours with the toys Papa brought home and not trouble Mamma who was delicate and who needed much rest.

Early one morning in May, Papa woke me.

"You must get dressed quickly," he said. "I will take you to Bubbie's house."

"Mamma?" I queried tremulously.

"Go with Papa, Sophela," she said softly. "I'll see you later."

When Papa brought me home again in the later afternoon, Mamma was still in bed. She lay propped up on the big, thick feather pillows that had been part of her dowry. A fresh white counterpane covered her bed. Her face was pale and her thick auburn hair was loosely plaited in a crown about her head. The room had a sweetish smell of disinfectant.

Auntie greeted me at the door.

"Come and see the new baby," she said. "See how pretty she is."

"See how small she is? Sleeping right there in your Mamma's arm…"

Timidly I glanced at the mystery called "baby." There she lay, a tiny red face with a fringe of orange hair. The eyes were shut and the tiny bud of a mouth was busy making sucking noises.

"This is your little sister Deenie," Mamma introduced us, expos-

Family photo with Shulamis, age eight, and Baby Deenie, 1921.
Jewish Public Library.

ing the infant's hand.

But even as I marvelled at the diminutive wonder, I withdrew instinctively from the rival who was claiming Mamma's attention.

"She's your little sister," Mamma repeated. "See her tiny fingers? See her tiny nose?"

All I could see was Mamma's love for the stranger who lay in her bed, in the place where I wanted to be but was not allowed.

A few days later I stood by the large front-parlour window looking out while Mamma sat in her rocker nursing the baby. Suddenly a large horse-drawn wagon drew up before our house. A huge man descended and pulled out two large, bulky packages wrapped in straw and brown paper.

Auntie, who had again dropped in to visit, let him in.

"Vichna, the furniture is here," she announced.

I looked on as the man unwrapped the cradle and the carriage we had seen in the store window. No, those things weren't for me. They were for the New Baby.

The following Sunday, as Mamma moved slowly about the house she said, "Today we are having a party. All the aunties are coming and we will throw candy into the baby's cradle and into her carriage so she will have a sweet life."

We stood by the cradle on the left side of the big bed. It was all white except for the red ribbons Mamma had tied on it to ward off the evil eye. There lay the baby dressed in the long cotton dimity dress Mamma had prepared in advance, a dress with dozens of tiny tucks alternating with narrow bands of fine lace and white ribbon. Mamma opened a large paper bag of cookies, sugar-dipped orange marmalade "ladies", and said, with a fond smile to the aunties and Papa and me, "Here. Take. Throw in the cradle. Our Deenie should have a sweet life."

"A sweet life! A sweet life!" they echoed, carefully throwing the candy into the cradle at the baby's feet.

"Now in the carriage," Papa urged, and the ceremony was repeated with the same words, "A sweet life! A sweet life!"

Only I remained distant and silent.

~

SCARLET FEVER

THE ONLY TIME I RECALL sitting on Mamma's knees was when I had scarlet fever.

I was four-and-a-half years old. I was wearing a white flannel nightdress with pink ribbon running through a band of eyelet embroidery about the neck and wrists. My tow-coloured hair was in curls and I felt very warm. I clung to Mamma as we sat by the parlour window in the late afternoon, the white lace curtain drawn aside. We were facing our family doctor as he drew the neckband of my nightgown down, examined my chest, and applied the stethoscope.

Our doctor was a gentle man, smaller than Papa. I recall him, in the afternoon greyness, a brown presence: his suit was brown, his tie was brown, the little buttons on his vest were brown, and his short hair was brown as was his small closely cropped moustache. Even his voice, which was somewhat high-pitched, had a soft, brown quality that seemed both odd and comforting to me.

As he folded away his stethoscope, he looked first to Mamma and then to me and said gently, "Sophela, would you like to go to the hospital?"

I clutched at Mamma's housedress, pressing my head against her breast. I didn't know what the word "hospital" meant, but I did know that I didn't want to go anywhere. I wanted to stay right where I was, on Mamma's lap, in our parlour by the window.

"With scarlet fever you have to go to the hospital," he explained.

I began to cry. I seemed to sense some scheme to separate me from this familiar place.

"Don't cry," he comforted me, trying to take my hand, which I drew away. "You will be with lots of other children. They, too, have to leave Mamma for a little while."

I looked at Mamma through tears. Was she willing to let me go? I looked at the crib in the corner of the other half of the double parlour where we all slept, and I trembled.

Was it because of that New Baby that I had to be sent away?

As if in answer to my unasked question, our doctor said, "You don't want the baby to get sick too, do you?"

What had my being sick to do with that New Baby? Ever since

she had come into our house I was reminded to step down and make room for That Baby! I cried even more profusely.

"Your Mamma will buy you a nice big doll, won't you Mamma?" the doctor cued her in.

I had lots of toys: a small table and a rocking chair, a large spinning top that hummed as it rotated, a painted wooden Russian doll-within-a doll-within-a-doll-within-a-doll, a round-bottomed Santa that rocked and rocked and didn't fall over – and there were many more small ones that the New Baby had broken. But a doll? Mamma always made one for me from a towel, nice and cuddly. That was my doll.

I pointed to my doll in the shoebox by the wall.

"Do you want a real doll?" he asked again.

For the moment I was distracted. "Yes," I answered, drying my eyes with my knuckles.

"Good," said the doctor and, turning to Mamma, he said, "Don't worry, Mrs. Borodensky. She'll be all right there. It's better for her in the hospital. You can't keep her at home."

I recall a strange husky man and a large red woolen blanket. I began to cry loudly as Mamma stepped away from my bed to let him wrap me and take me away.

The rest comes back in the light of a nightmare: Papa and Mamma were standing by the open doors of the long black ambulance while the man strapped me to the stretcher inside. No words were spoken, no one was crying. Even I was not crying. I was two children: I was the observer intrigued by the ongoing ceremony, and I was the victim, anguished by my expulsion from our home.

As the heavy doors closed, leaving me in inner darkness, I cried again. Was it right I should be ejected from that house because of the New Baby, that I should leave my place and familiar things to her, and without a word or sound accept this exile to an unknown place via that long block wagon?

Turning my head, I saw beside me the large head of a lifeless doll. I knew I wouldn't love her. Despite her dark eyes and black hair, I saw her as that pink and white red-headed baby who slept in the crib on the other side of the big bed, in the back parlour, That Baby who had made me again a stranger.

What happened to the doll? I don't recall ever seeing her again.

Did I reject her after that first night or did she become part of the communal toy chest in the children's ward of St. Paul's Hospital for Communicable Diseases? I don't know, and in the totally new surroundings, I don't recall ever longing for her or remembering her with love.

I still feel the dark red aura of that ward. Perhaps it was in the two long lines of small white iron cots, each with a wooden chair beside it, and the mysterious floating motion of the black-garbed, hooded nuns with their white coifs who tended to us.

I recall the first morning I was allowed off the bed to wash myself: the small stepladder I had to mount to reach the sink, the brushing of my teeth with the Forhan's toothpaste Mamma had provided, and the sweet-tasting Dobell's tablet in a gargle we were encouraged to use each day.

I recall kneeling in prayer at the nun's feet to repeat the words in a language I did not understand, and the smiling face of the Little Sister who taught me how to roll my hair ribbons on the lower wooden rung of the chair so they would be straight and ready for wear again the next day.

I recall the admonition of the nuns as they hurried us into bed and put out all the lights except the small night light at the end of the hall. "Vatkooshay perkon veezeet," ("Vas te coucher parce qu'on visite") we repeated, laughing as we hurried into bed. What it meant I didn't know, but it sounded auspicious.

I recall, too, the Bigger Boy in the running shoes who plagued me when I was lonely, who said that my brown wrapper and carpet slippers were bought from a rag peddler, and although I knew he was wrong, yet, might he not be right? For what could one expect from a mother who stood quietly by as they took her child in a huge red blanket and tied her onto a board with wide straps in a black wagon which took her from her own bed, her home, and all that was familiar?

I never grew accustomed to the ward. A small brown wrapper-clad child with ribbon-plaited hair, I walked sadly between the rows of beds in my carpet slippers, humming little tunes to myself.

The days Mamma came to visit were the hardest. Did other

parents come too? I don't know. I only know I was invited to the open window, and there below, just off the green lawn with its bright geranium beds, stood Mamma in her dark skirt and white silk blouse, smiling and waving to me. I felt nothing. Once my Bubbie stood with her, my Bubbie in her black Sabbath dress and peruke. She didn't smile. Her white hands were folded and she looked up at me. I felt a rush of love.

Later the little Sister unwrapped a package by my bed.

"Your Mamma asked if she could bring something. We told her to bring a Bible with your name in it so we could pray for you." I could picture my Bubbie at her Sabbath candles, covering her eyes as she prayed.

Why can't I recall the moment when I was told I would be going home? Surely that must have evoked some feeling in me. I recall sitting on top of the small ladder in the ward washroom as the Little Sister dressed me and combed out my hair. A small smile passed between us. She was my friend. As she pulled the freshly unrolled ribbon through my hair, tugging it to and fro to make it just right, I felt another tug – a movement within me, tugging me to and fro…

Mamma met me downstairs. She smiled and took my hand and we walked out onto the pavement between the lawns and the flowerbeds to go home. Because it was Saturday, Papa could not come. It was his busiest day at the store.

On Sunday afternoon, the young aunts and uncles came to celebrate my homecoming. There were presents and smiles and we all had tea. I sat with them at the table, silent, my inward eye at the hospital. I could not help wondering what the Little Sister and the Bigger Boy were doing then.

[At age four and a half Shulamis was hospitalized with scarlet fever for nine-and-a-half weeks in St. Paul's Hospital for Contagious Diseases. It was established in 1905 as the contagious ward of Notre-Dame Hospital, near Montreal's Parc La Fontaine.]

I FIND MY JEWISH NAME

ONE WINTRY SUNDAY NIGHT I found myself with my parents and other members of the family in the Monument National Theatre on St. Lawrence Boulevard, The Main. We were attending the graduation exercises of the Jewish Peretz Shule, the afternoon Yiddish school then known as the *Natzionale Radikale Shule.* The auditorium was packed with parents, friends, and well-wishers, and a special production had been mounted for the occasion: a musical rendition of *Joseph and his Brethren.*

On stage, in the semi-darkness, the world of the Bible opened before me. There in the green fields of Canaan, amid sheaves of corn, Joseph the Dreamer appeared in his Coat of Many Colours and was denounced by his brothers for his arrogant dreams. The lights changed and in a torrid flow of colour the unwitting Joseph was attacked by those jealous brothers who threw him into the pit to die, his glorious coat rent and defiled with animal blood to deceive his devastated, loving father.

The boy pleaded for mercy, but the wicked brothers were adamant, and poor Joseph was left alone, his anguished voice rising out of the pit as the malevolent men turned away. Only the fortuitous arrival of a caravan – so the singing voice of Reuben told us – saved the day, and he, Reuben, the eldest, pleaded with the others to sell the lad to the traders lest Joseph's blood be on their heads.

I was in another world as scene after scene filled the stage with colour, music, and heart-rending melodrama. Finally, the performance drew to a close as the Viceroy Joseph, in his purple cloak and golden coronet, enfolded his beloved father in his arms and offered forgiveness to his amazed, repentant brothers – and the curtain fell.

The audience went wild with applause. Exultant fathers and mothers ran to the stage with bouquets of flowers and boxes of candy for their so-gifted progeny, much to the anguish of those others who were not so rewarded for their efforts. The crowd milled around, everyone congratulating everyone else on the success of the evening. I clung to my Mamma's arm as something in me thundered, "This is mine! This is mine! I, too, must one day be a part of the wonderful world of the *Shule*."

Shulamis, Deenie (to her left), and Arele (dark shirt) and friends, on
Coloniale Avenue which led through the backyard to the Peretz Shule.
Jewish Public Library.

In my Bubbie's house that memory was constantly reinforced
by the Yiddish songs sung by my young aunts and uncles, songs
they brought home from the *Shule* or from the Jewish culture clubs
they attended. I pleaded with Mamma to let me go to *Shule* too, and
great was my joy when she told me one September morning in my
eighth year that I was to go to *Shule* now.

I could hardly wait for the afternoon at Strathearn School to
come to an end. I ran home, rushed through my snack of milk and
bread and jam, and heart high I floated all the way to *Shule* to attend
my four o'clock class.

In the twilit room I took my place beside another little girl at
a wooden double-desk. Before us on the wall hung an enormous
photograph of a large moustached gentleman with deep dark eyes
and a wise, friendly smile. He wore a black-buttoned coat with
narrow lapels and a stiff white collar. A tuft of dark hair fell over his
high forehead towards his shaggy right eyebrow. I liked him at once.

"Who is this?" I nudged my small neighbour.

"That's Mr. Peretz. It's his school."

The teacher, a winsome young woman with smiling eyes, greeted us in Yiddish from her platform. "Some of you were not here when classes started the other day so I'll repeat what I told the class then," she said.

She told us that her name was *Lereren* Sherr. "*Lereren* means a lady teacher," she explained. Then she went on to say how glad she was to have so many new children in her class and promised that we would have a good time together and learn many things. She pointed to the picture of the nice man on the wall.

"This is the great Yiddish writer, Yitschak Labish Peretz, for whom the school was named. He is no longer alive, but he wrote many wonderful poems and stories in his lifetime. You will learn some of them, just as he hoped you would." I felt she was speaking directly to me. "And perhaps, some day," she continued, "you, too, will write wonderful poems and stories for other children to enjoy."

I swallowed her every word, her every gesture. Here I belonged. If only the classes weren't held so late in the day!

"Now," said *Lereren* Sherr, "I will call the roll and you will answer *Doh*, which means 'Present'. If you attended the singing class on Saturday afternoon you will say *Geven*, which means that you were there. And if you have your homework, you will say *Gemacht*. Remember: *Doh, geven, gemacht*."

"Dovid?"

"*Doh, gemacht*."

"Channah?"

"*Doh, geven, gemacht*."

"Baile?"

"*Doh, geven, gemacht*."

"Raizl?"

"*Doh*."

"Chaim?"

"*Doh, gemacht*."

"Sophie?"

There was a lull. It was me she was calling but I could not answer. Everyone had a Jewish name but I! For what sort of Jewish name was Sophie or even Sophele? I burst into tears, my head on the wooden desk.

The teacher and the children were distressed. "What's the matter?" everyone asked. "Are you not feeling well?" *Lereren* Sherr wanted to know.

"No," I wailed. "I – don't have a Jewish name!"

The children looked at one another in dismay. Miss Sherr came down from her platform. Her gentle voice encompassed me. "Don't cry," she comforted me, an arm around my shoulder. "I'm sure you have a Jewish name. Ask your mother."

At home I looked accusingly into Mamma's eyes. "Everyone in *Shule* has a Jewish name except me!" I attacked. "Sophele! Sophele!" I scoffed at myself bitterly.

"But of course you have a Jewish name!" Mamma replied. "Your name is Shulamis, for my father Shloime."

"Then why do you call me Sophele?"

"We live in Canada. We wanted you to have an English name for school. Sophia was a famous woman, a Russian socialist..."

But who cared for Russia, for Socialism, for Fame?

Shulamis! Shulamis! The air was filled with music as I repeated it again and again. I was no longer an outcast in my own heart. I belonged and I had a Jewish name like all other children in the class – and such a lovely singing name!

In *Shule* next day, as I brought the glad tidings to the class, I was several cubits taller.

"*Shulamis*?" said the teacher. "What a lovely name! Shulamis is the sweetheart of King Solomon in the *Shir Hashirim*, the Song of Songs."

There was mixed reaction to her reply. Some of the children remained wide-eyed, open-mouthed with wonder, others sniggered...

And I? I was transported with joy and unfathomable memory! And while I was in the Protestant school I continued to be known as Sophie, I was *Shulamis*, she of the singing name, the little girl who lived on Coloniale Avenue near Prince Arthur and the Sweetheart of King Solomon.

A new dimension was added to my life. Within the walls of the *Shule* I learned that the Sabbath was for singing, and that before my ancestors lived in Russia I had ancestors who had lived in Spain, in Babylon, in Egypt, and in the golden Promised Land. There, too, I learned of a return to Zion, of lasting friendships, of responsibility to the community in which I lived, and of love. From the thread that started spinning on that magical night in the Monument National Theatre, I began to weave a Coat of Many Colours of my own.

∼

PAPA FINDS A COUNTRY

EVERY SPRING PAPA made his pilgrimage to the Laurentian Mountains "to find a country."

Soon after Passover, when the snow had begun to disappear and the days grew longer, Mamma would begin her incantation, "Soon will be summer. Where will we go? We have to look for a *kontra*. We have to find a place for the summer…"

On the first promising Sunday, Papa would take the nine a.m. train from Mile End Station and go as far as Ste. Agathe. He would hunt in and around the neighbouring villages of the Jewish summer ghetto, seeking out farmers who rented out cottages or moved into their summer kitchens for the season and rented out their own houses for whatever they would bring.

Since there was no transportation in these little villages, it was important to rent from a farmer who could undertake to supply his tenants with fresh milk, eggs, and vegetables from his own farm. There was also the anticipation for the buggy ride Mamma would arrange for us with the farmer once a year, a treat that always made the summer memorable.

That Sunday morning, Mamma sent Papa off with the usual catalogue of specific instructions.

"Remember, Philip: a new house. With a good stove. And the pump should work easy. And it should be near the train and near the river for swimming. And not too deep for the children. And not too far from the village; they should be able to go for mail every day. And with a good farmer with a horse and buggy – he should deliver and take us sometimes for a drive…"

My little sister Deenie and I stood by, full of excitement. She was a loving little girl and I had grown very protective of her. As the day ahead seemed endless to us, I said, "Deenie, let's go play outside."

We joined the children on the street. My friends Bessie and Sarah were trying to play skipping with another girl. The boys kept interfering, jumping in to "catch a free skip." Bessie was threatening them with the rope. "Get away from here, ya hear? I'll smack ya with the handles!" We ran to join in the fun.

Deenie couldn't contain herself. "Our father's gone to look for a country!" she announced.

"So?" said Bessie, raising her chin defiantly. "He finds you a country and you miss all the fun in the city!"

But Deenie didn't hear. "It's so good there..." she rambled on. "It's green all over and smells so good with Christmas trees!"

"Yeh, sure!" scoffed Bessie enviously again.

"You have fun here and we have fun there," I countered. "You remember last year I sent you a letter on birch bark from the trees there? And we made a concert with the other children and we danced "Ring Around the Rosie" and sang "The Make Belief Forever" just like in school by the gym concert..."

"All right! All right! Ya wanna skip or no?" Bessie cut us off. "You and Sarah take an end. I'll skip first." And as she turned rope, she began to intone, acting out the rhyme as she skipped.

Teddy Bear Teddy Bear
turn around.
Teddy Bear Teddy Bear
touch the ground
Teddy Bear Teddy Bear
show your shoe
Teddy Bear Teddy Bear
One-two-three skidoo!

"Now pepper!" she shouted.

I quickened the rope. "Faster! Faster!" she shouted. The rope smacked the sidewalk with the speed of an egg-beater. Suddenly Sarah called, "Bessie, you're out! You're next, Sophie."

Even as I skipped, I was out there somewhere with Papa on the

66

train, on the country roads viewing the empty summer cottages that were waiting for us and for other children to bring them to life.

"Sophie Borodensky, what's the matter with you!" Bessie's bark suddenly cut the air. "It's *pepper* already! You're out!"

Toward evening, Papa returned exhausted but content.

"I found a *kontra*," he reported. "A beauty. New. In Belisle's Mills. Near the river. Not far from the train. A sandy beach. Good for swimming and a few houses for neighbours. And not far from a hotel…"

We all smiled happily at him.

"How many rooms?" asked Mamma.

"How many rooms?" Papa hesitated. "Seven," he finally said.

Mamma's eyes bulged. "Seven rooms!? Madness! Madness – on my enemies' heads! I need seven rooms? I'll kill myself!"

"It's a beautiful house. The best I saw," Papa pleaded.

Mamma was livid. "So? I need seven rooms? What will I do with them? Who'll clean them?"

"You'll rent out two rooms, like by other people."

"I need *tenners*? Women around the stove?" Mamma clasped her hands in consternation. "Such a big house! Who'll look after it?"

"This is the last time I go look for a *kontra!*" Papa exploded in one of the few times I heard him raise his voice. He threw himself into a heap on the large red-leather armchair. "I do my best to please you. I come back tired like a dog and you're not satisfied! You'll hire a girl and you'll take the children and you'll go to the *kontra* – or else stay home! I'm finished, you hear! Finished!"

Mamma sulked for a day, then spoke on the phone for the next couple of days and rented out two rooms to two ladies with good recommendations from other ladies with whom they had previously shared houses. "If they can get along with them, so can I," she announced. "I can get along with anyone!" And she gave Papa a meaningful look.

We waited eagerly for the school year to come to an end. The day school let out, a truck picked up our trunks, and the next morning at nine, Mamma, Deenie, and I and the newly hired maid, Winnie, boarded the train for Val David, Quebec, then known as Belisle's Mills.

This was the first of many wonderful summers in Belisle's Mills.

Oh, those summers with the Laurentian Mountains gently ringing the valley like a porridge bowl, rainbows and sunsets throwing stained-glass reflections on their green craggy sides, fragrant fields of hay and clover, wild flowers unnamed until I had named them. There was always that first taste of wild strawberries (*zemlieniki*, Mamma called them), and the raspberries, blueberries, and black-berries that appeared in succession for our pleasure during the eight weeks we spent there, and the fragrance of the boiling fruit turning to jam or jelly on the wood stove, liquid sunshine which filled the many quarts of tightly sealed mason jars which Papa took every Sunday night to fill the pantry shelves for our winter's delight! Zaida always spent part of the summer with us, as did our young aunts who came for their vacation.

We grew and flourished. I improved my swimming; Deenie learned to swim. We rose early and went to bed with the birds. The farmer kept his promise and delivered fresh vegetables, mild and often still warm eggs. Mamma rested in the afternoon sun and enjoyed the companionship of the other women while we played with the children in the yard. On Tuesday mornings Mamma would say, "Today we write letters to Papa," and she wrote the same letter every week:

Dear Philip,
    We are well and hope to hear the same from you. Everything here is the same. Please bring with you when you come…

Then followed the list of the many things he should bring. I, in her image, added our letter.

Dear Papa,
    We are well. We're having a good time. How are you? Please bring us…

On Saturday night Papa arrived with two heavy valises full of fruit and other seasonal delectables, supplies which we could not get in the country store or from the farmer. There was always the box of Laura Secord chocolates, one piece to be enjoyed after lunch every day instead of the two cents for candy we received at home during the school year. Papa would join us for berry picking, swimming, and at all our meals. How good it was to be together.

"I wish summer could be forever," Deenie often whispered at the end of such days. "Me too," I nodded, already looking to the next weekend.

As I look back, all those summers fade into one nostalgic sameness, a sameness broken only by the awareness of the lengthening of our shoes, of the budding of our breasts, and of the slow awakening of girlhood hungers as well as their potential aftermath. Like the aftermath of that first summer which had brought us Winnie, through whom we learned that there was loud joyous laughter, and also that there was sorrow in the world.

⁓

WINNIE

WINNIE WAS THE FIRST of a long line of maids who stayed with us in my childhood home. Finding the right maid wasn't easy, but Mamma was always ailing and someone had to do the housework, shop for things that were not delivered to the house, and, in general, do Mamma's bidding. Winnie shared our room; she slept in the single bed by the window and Deenie and I shared a three-quarter bed.

She came to us at the end of May, about a month before we went to the country that summer. I didn't take to Winnie. She was a big, strapping country girl from New Brunswick who spoke only French, laughed loudly and heartily, and offered up prayers to a strange God who favoured rosary beads and crosses – a totally different God from my Grandmother's. Winnie came on the heels of a girl who had been dismissed after her first afternoon in our house. She had locked herself in the bathroom for a long time and Mamma was worried.

"Find out what she's doing there so long," urged my Auntie who had dropped in for an afternoon cup of tea. "You don't know who she is. After all, you have young children in the house…"

When the girl came out of the bathroom carrying a rubber bag with a long tube and a box of medication in her hands, Mamma was doubly distressed. She phoned the druggist, Mr. Schmerling, who sent his message boy for the medication, and I later heard Mamma tell Papa over the phone, "He says it's a medicine for women who have to do with men."

"In that case," said Papa (as I again heard Mamma tell my Auntie), "Pay her for the next day and tell her to go right away."

The next day Mamma hired Winnie.

Winnie came with clear demands: she would be paid twenty dollars a month, have Thursday afternoons and second Sundays off, and be free to go home for Christmas with pay.

When I told my friend Bessie that we had a French maid, she bristled. "Why French? They hate the Jews worse than the English. They're Cath'lics – like the nuns. Why doesn't your mother get English – you should be able to talk to her?"

"They don't answer the advertisement. Only the French. That's why. And my father says there's good and bad people by everyone. And anyways, I could learn French."

Winnie's large white teeth and hearty laugh frightened me, but Mamma took to her, except that she was horrified by Winnie's appetite. "I just bought a half-peck apples yesterday by Mr. Umansky," she told Papa the next day, "and they're all gone already. And a half *kimmel* bread with butter and jam she ate up this afternoon with tea…"

"Leave her," said Papa, remembering his hungry days as an apprentice to a tailor in the Old Country. "She'll eat till she's full, then she'll stop. You'll see."

Hard as it was for Mamma, she controlled herself and Winnie stayed on because she worked well and made Mamma laugh – without language, but with funny gestures. She quickly picked up some words from Mamma's defective English and before long we felt that Winnie was here to stay.

In Belisle's Mills Winnie was in her element. She loved the country. She never seemed to be lonely. She was cheerful, sang her French-Canadian songs, and loved to whistle. She was a magician with the wood stove despite the early-morning damp wood, and was a whizz at priming the pump and getting the wicks in the coal-oil lamps to burn without smoking. Our wooden floors shone under her mop and the other women appreciated her help. She soon made friends with the French-Canadian help at the nearby Jewish hotel and at the end of every day, she made her way through the woods to laugh with the young folk who spoke her language and belonged to her class.

Deenie and I had little to do with her. She was our mother's maid and that was that. She slept in the large unfinished attic, and we were never allowed to intrude into her domain. We were just as happy not to, for we had heard the flapping of wings up there and we were scared as Winnie – who didn't know the English name for the creatures – laughed her loud toothsome laugh, ogled us with wide protruding eyes, flapped her hands, thumbs close to her temples, and made a strange muffled sound.

"Bats," Mamma said. "Madame Dufresne says bats fly around here and sometimes they hide in the attic in dark corners."

"She'll have to cut off all her hair!" I cried, covering my own with hands, in horror, as I remembered the rhyme I had picked up from the other children:

Bats in the hair –
no longer fair…

Winnie laughed. "Me no 'fraid," she spoke her newly acquired phrases. "Me ketch'm coup coup!" she continued, motioning two sharp blows with the edge of her palm on the creatures' imaginary necks. "Puis – bam-bam – sur la porte. Bonne chance. For luck!" she roared again. I shuddered as I recalled the spread-winged mouse-like creatures on Farmer Dufresne's barn door.

I envied Winnie. I envied her lusty laughter, her ability to make Mamma laugh, her grown-up fun with the farmer's son, Jehoshaphat, and her general ease in the world. Mamma's constant ailing had turned me inward and I envied Winnie so much that one day I stole seven cents from her purse. I was too frightened to spend it and threw it into the river, but Winnie was aware of the robbery and let me know she knew. While she said nothing to Mamma, there existed a terrible bond between us.

On Thursday afternoons, Mamma played bridge at the Jewish hotel. The games were arranged to raise funds for Jewish charities.

There was a shortcut through the forest from our house to the hotel. It was a lovely trodden path, bordered by wild ferns, tall pines, and birches, with soft green turf and red berries cushioning the ground on both sides. To others it was only a shortcut, but to me it was a magical road.

Each time I walked along the path I mesmerized myself by peering up high into the treetops to see where the sun hung, or by searching out the stars and the changing moon. Whenever my eyes returned to the path again, I was sure I would meet a wonderful stranger as in the Fairy Tales I was reading – not necessarily on a white horse on such a narrow path, but a fine stranger – a Prince who would tell me of his wanderings and would be able to solve all riddles. We couldn't be married, right away, nor could he take me at once to his far-off castle, but he would leave me with a promise that in a few years, when he had solved his three riddles . . . It was a lovely place.

One Thursday afternoon, Mamma had gone to attend the weekly fund-raising bridge party at the hotel. It was also Winnie's afternoon off. I had stayed around the house playing with the other children. As dusk began to fall, I had suddenly grown wistful and decided to go find Mamma.

As I entered the woods, I thought I heard a low moaning. I stopped and listened. It wasn't a bird; it wasn't the wind. I could see nothing. The moaning stopped for a short while and I continued into the woods.

Suddenly it started again in waves of growing intensity and I was frightened. I looked back to find I was more than halfway through the woods. I couldn't turn back. As I took a step forward, I let out a wild shriek. There, behind a copse in the twilight, was a ghost – a real ghost – waving its arms heavy with flowing whiteness and moaning, moaning in terrifying anguish, "OOOOOOOOO! Ooooooooo! OOOOOOOOOO!"

I froze in my steps. "Mamma! Mamma!" I shrieked in unfamiliar tones. "Mamma! Mamma!"

The ghost seemed to take a step toward me. "Monee…Monee," the ghost wailed at me!

"No! No more!" I shrieked again. "Mamma! Mamma!"

A roar of laughter filled the air. It was Winnie, robed in a sheet. "Jus' pour le fun!" she roared. "Don' yell! C'est jus' pour le fun!" And she came forward, pulling off the sheet and laughing wildly.

She took me home and fed me cold milk with bread and jam.

When Mamma came home I was in bed. My eyes were red with crying.

"What happened?" Mamma asked. Winnie stood behind her, smiling in the doorway.

"It was dark in the shortcut and I got frightened…But Winnie came and took me home."

"There's nothing to be afraid of in these woods, is there Winnie?" Mamma asked, looking first at me and then at the smiling maid.

"No. Never. Just ghosts!" And she roared again.

Silently I shook my head. We were even and I was free.

~

WHO SAYS YOU CAN'T GO HOME AGAIN?

~ Diary Entry – return to the old house, Thursday 3/16/84

[Edited to include excerpts from the preface of the 1983 edition of *Shulamis: Stories from a Montreal Childhood*]

In 1984, I showed Gilah around the Prince Arthur area, the Shulamis Area.

Many of my early landmarks were still there, although somewhat changed: Fletcher's Field (now Jeanne-Mance Park), St.Urban (now St.Urbain) Street, my old schools, Strathearn Elementary and Baron Byng High School (now home to Sun Youth), and Bancroft School where I had spent my first four years as a teacher of grade two.

The Main (St-Laurent Boulevard) was my old home territory. Here I had run errands for my mother, and had once received from Cape's Pharmacy a silver-plated coffee spoon as a premium with a purchase of a half-pound of chocolates. Across the road was the dry goods store where a school friend had lived. On Prince Arthur

Street where we had walked to Strathearn School every school day, the north side was quite intact, although the south side was almost all restaurants. At #63 was the old Prince Arthur Hall, the place of union meetings, weddings, and lectures. This was where I had heard Eugene V. Debs, Papa's idol. I was seven years old and I don't recall what he said, but I do remember he was a rather slight man in a brown suit. This hall even served as a synagogue during the Jewish High Holidays, where those unaffiliated with a particular synagogue could come and worship for a three-cent ticket. The fruit store was once Rosen's Fruit Store, and around the corner at Colonial (now Coloniale) Street was the house where I lived.

The house still stood with its winding metal outdoor stairs and handsome bay windows, freshly painted and still in beautiful condition. It was no longer 128a but 3638 Coloniale. We had lived in the middle flat of this three-story building attached by a balcony and a median wall to its replica on the left.

We stopped in front of my house on Coloniale (3638 – 128a) & I said, "I've been wanting to go in & see what it looks like to me now."

Gilah refused. Was shocked that I'd "invade" without an appointment.

"Leave your phone number and a note & if they want you they'll call." So civilized.

When I mentioned it later to my friend Dana, she said, "Let's do it." And we headed back again to the old neighbourhood.

We held on to the wrought iron banister as we mounted the wooden steps. "One winter, when I was a child, I slipped down these snow-packed stairs and landed on 'my dignity.' The stairs were packed with snow and I was busy daydreaming about being a famous actress."

We had all laughed.

I recognized the brass bell, the brass doorknob, and the letter slot I had polished every Friday after school.

There is no answer to my repeated ring, but there is a Portuguese family living upstairs in the Schneiderman flat (3636). "We were wondering if we could go in and see the flat," I offered. "I lived here when I was a little girl, and my friend and I would like to see the

"The house still stood with its winding metal outdoor stairs and handsome bay windows." The Borodensky's flat was on the right.
Photo by Gilah Yelin Hirsch.

house. I wrote a book of stories about my childhood here."

The daughter let us in saying, "It's empty." After the fire (in the old Malo house) the walls had been gutted. (A woman had been burnt there, alas. I heard about the fire on the radio.) The firemen were worried about cinders & had broken through.

"The fire didn't reach these flats but they were black from smoke. We just had it completely repainted and now it's for rent. You're welcome to come in and see."

This was far beyond my wildest dream. My memories would not be encumbered by other people's possessions! I wondered what changes had been made in the house over the years.

From the hall, I stepped into the parlour.

I could see the red leather chesterfield with the large leather arm-chairs in their places. I remember Papa had slept on the couch & made a bed for Pesach Arele with the 2 large chairs at night and the bay windows thru which the moon in the curtains threw patterns. How many tenants had entertained guests in that room? The softwood floors were freshly painted red, and the bay window still had its built-in window seat covering the radiator coils. I recalled the fringed leather pillow with maple leaves and red-clad Mounted Police painted on it, the gas-lit fireplace in the wall facing the doorway, and the figured rug. Above it all was the chandelier I recalled so clearly. There it was – the frosted pressed-glass bowl still holding the light bulbs.

The memories flooded back and I was home again!

The hall curved to make a large closet under the upper floor's stairs, the place where we kept our summer things – country trunks, etc. On the right, the radiators above which had hung the large wooden framed hall mirror, with hooks on which we hung our hats, coats, etc. Behind that mirror I had hidden the baby's photo, after his death to keep Mamma from looking at it constantly & crying. For my desire to protect her I was rewarded with a roll of curses when I finally took it out & returned it. They used that photo on his tombstone, where I still see it in its gold and ivory frame. I <u>know</u> it wasn't because I was jealous of the child that I hid it. I really couldn't bear Mamma's constant crying as she sat & looked at it. I know too, that I was accusing her of being melodramatic, as I often did. I was 12 when he died from meningitis – a sudden illness that lasted only 10 days.

Strange how removed I was already then. That new baby was no threat to me: he was <u>theirs</u>, Papa tended to him at night, Mamma by day. I don't recall that we had a maid at that time. Or did we have Lucienne then?

Mamma's bedroom. So small! I don't recall their double bed in that room, but I do recall the beautiful new mahogany bureau & the 2 twin beds & the "vanity". Papa says he kept the highboy in the basement of his shop until we moved. I do recall the new twin beds, because I remember Leon Gold, the actor and a friend of the family, making cute-lewd comment like, "So? Now it's all over, is it? No more?" Just as, while Mamma was pregnant, he kept joking, "Need any help? Perhaps a little toe, or an ear is still missing?" etc.

(Can it be that people really didn't yet know that a baby is fully created? I remember thinking how funny it was that he should suggest adding bits & pieces, yet I wondered.)

Nothing had been changed.

The old toilet & bath & small sink with the bit of oilcloth on the floor, all intact, the one holy private place where no one could barge in after you, where I hid from Gold when I was hysterical because he was leaving.

Our bedroom, where Deenie & I and Winnie slept, Di & I in the 3 quarter bed, Winnie on a cot or quarter bed, - room for everyone in that small room; the walls where I arranged displays of the drawings I brought home at term's end (where but in school, had I ever seen that?) and the electric cord with its lampshade-covered bulb that hung from the ceiling. Small lampshade – that was the clue to the near kidnapping when I was twelve. (A man had scaled the post to our second-storey balcony, had come in through that window & was lifting me in his arms when I awoke. No, it wasn't a dream. The lampshade was covered with my panties!)

How privileged I was that the house was empty & freshly painted, and I could place my furniture as I remembered it! The dining room still has a chandelier, but it's not the one I knew, it's a modern fashion one like the one I have in my bedroom now. But there [against] the wall I could see the china cabinet with its two pressed-glass fruit compotes & its leaded doors behind which stood Papa's books; the window beside which stood "the lounge" & later Mamma's sewing machine at which I sat to write my novel, "Beth Belmont of the Storms". And the door leading to the "gallery" where Rita & I made the lacy wand for one of our plays.

But the most nostalgic surprise was the kitchen. It was exactly as I remembered it. But it was smaller – the small wooden cupboards above & below the old sink where on Saturdays I scrubbed & polished Mamma's copper fish pot; the "table" - that old washtub with the board on it as it had been, where we discussed whether or not I should "take" scripture. The furnace! The furnace was still there, but it had shrunk! And it had some kind of heat control mechanism on it! I could still see the flames devouring the pages of Maria Monk"s, *Little Blue Book* that Hilda Abrahams had brought for us to read! Shabby oilcloth on the floor.

The pantry. The pantry hadn't been cleaned or repaired, except that where we'd had coal they had stacked logs of firewood for the fireplace they'd put into the living room. The space for the icebox was the same, but 2 men were putting in a refrigerator where it had stood!

In a word, the place had been retained as a <u>Museum for Shulamis</u>! Only the rent had changed. Where we had paid $28, they were asking $325.00 plus self-heating.

Once again as I went out I stopped to fondle the brass doorbell, letterbox slot & door handle I used to polish with Brasso every Friday after school . . .

∼

DEENIE PREPARES FOR SCHOOL

THAT SUMMER, DEENIE just couldn't wait for the season to end.

"When will it be Labour Day already?" she kept asking. Neither the fresh young corn from our farmer's garden, nor the heavy crop of wild blackberries that flourished that summer, could compensate. Even Mamma's repeated praise as she quickly converted our take into jars and jars of purple-red translucent jelly didn't satisfy. As the August rains came down and the houses emptied of their summer guests, Deenie asked the same question every day: "When will it be Labour Day?" It's getting so empty in the yard…"

"It's better in the country," Mamma said. "The air is fresh – and we paid until Labour Day."

Papa brought a calendar and Mamma invited Deenie to cross off each day as bedtime came around.

"See? Not so long already," Mamma finally announced. "Sunday, Papa will help us pack, and Monday is Labour Day and we go home."

"And Tuesday," Deenie rejoined, "we go write me into school!"

"May it be in a lucky hour!" Mamma blessed devoutly.

"I'll take you," I volunteered. "I'll take you to the office and *enroll* you," I corrected her Yiddishism.

During that last week, ours was the only inhabited house in the area. Fortunately the weather had turned hot and clear and we spent most of our time swimming or visiting the empty cottages in search of possible treasures the occupants might have left behind. Thus the week ran by more quickly than we had expected and on Labour Day, our arms laden with Golden Glow, the gift from our farmer who had come to say goodbye, we boarded the noon train for the pleasant journey home.

Some of the leaves on the maple across from our house were already turning red. As we got out of the taxi, the hot smell of the dusty street hit us. We looked about for our friends. The street was deserted. On some of the stoops before open doors, grey-faced neighbours sat scantily clad, waiting for the evening to bring a reprieving wind.

Suddenly, a familiar, raucous voice cut the air.

"Sarah, hey! Look who's here!" Bessie was waving to us from her stairs. "It's Sophie and Deenie back from the country!" We waved back happily.

"Boy! Ya missed some summer!" she called as they came running toward us.

"You look so sunburnt!" Sarah admired. "You had fun in the country?"

"Yeh." We were delighted to see our friends. "We had fun. You?"

Deenie bubbled over. "We went swimming and picked berries. It was nice there."

"Too bad your mother is always sick and you always have to go to the country. Ya missed *some* fun here," Bessie tantalized us to assuage her envy. "We went on Fletcher's Field every Sunday. We took a picnic: hard eggs and chicken and bread and jam. And my mother took the samovar for tea. We had fun…"

"And the other days?" I asked, not knowing how much to envy her.

"It wasn't so much fun," Sarah contradicted her. "It was hot and sticky and even if we went to Schubert's Bath (public swimming pool) on Main Street, it was still hot! I'm glad you were in the country," she added lovingly.

"Maybe next year you could come, too…" I offered, putting my arm around my friend's shoulder. "Next year we could have fun together."

"We came home to write me in school tomorrow," Deenie's smile lit all her freckles to a glow. "I have to go into kindergarten."

"Ya mean we have to *enroll* you," Bessie corrected as I had done. "Good. So we'll all go with you to the office in the morning."

"Bessie! You know the office teacher won't let…" Sarah intervened. "You know only those that *need* could go to the office. It gets too crowdy."

"So all right. We'll walk together to school in the morning," Bessie compromised. "But you should be early, ya hear? I want to be first in line. Eight o'clock. Ya hear?"

Deenie lit up again. The whole world revolved around her.

In the morning Deenie prodded me.

"Sophie, you're asleep?"

"Yeh. What time is it?" I heard her as though through a dream.

"I look nice?" she asked.

"What time is it?" My eyes were still shut. "The alarm went off already?"

"It didn't have to. I was awake."

I opened one eye and glanced at the clock. "Deenie, it's not even seven o'clock yet! Why are you dressed so early? Come to bed!"

"I can't! I have on my new school dress and my patent leather shoes. I couldn't sleep so I got dressed. It's in the morning already. We have to go to school to *enroll* me. Remember?" Deenie emphasized the word to show she remembered.

"It's so early! I want to sleep yet." I retreated under the covers.

"Sophie," she prodded me lightly again. "You remember today you have to write me in?" The repressed excitement in her voice touched me. I rubbed my eyes and sat up in bed.

"You look so nice, Deenie," I smiled through the morning blur. "The teacher will like you…"

As I brushed my teeth I heard Papa fixing the cocoa for our breakfast. Mamma in her green and yellow bathrobe joined me in the bathroom.

"It's a nice sunny day," she said softly, "I can't believe it. Already both my children in school. The house will be empty."

Through the open windows we heard the excitement on the street. "Not yet eight o'clock," Mamma noted. "What's their hurry? They should only want to go to school like this later in the year…"

Deenie was too excited to eat. "I can't. My belly feels funny!" she pleaded.

"You have to eat. A person has to have strength for school. You see the surprise Papa made for you? Cocoa and French toast. Eat. Eat. A new beginning is a special occasion. You have to treat it with respect."

"Mamma, let her just drink the cocoa," I tried to hurry them along from the doorway. "She should take the French toast for recess." Deenie gave me a mournful look as she gulped down the hot drink.

Mamma couldn't seem to let Deenie go. Every time she said goodbye and reached for the door, Mamma called her back.

"*Dinyela*, I'll fix your bow in the back of the dress."

"*Dinyela*, you forgot your hanky. Come, I'll pin it on for you."

"*Dinyela*, your hair ribbon isn't straight. A suchy year on me, on us all – like the sun shines on your golden head…"

I grew impatient. "Mamma, it's past eight already! They won't wait for us."

There was a struggle for control in Mamma's voice. "It's only eight o'clock!" she managed, adding sadly, "The time flies…both children in school already…" She walked to the door calling after us, "Go in good health! You should both have a good year, dear God. It should be a good beginning! We should all be well and Papa and I should only have pleasure from you…"

∾

I UNROLL DEENIE IN SCHOOL

"BESSIE, WAIT FOR ME! I'm coming!" I shouted from our balcony to my friend who was already walking away.

"You're slow like molasses! I'm not waiting!" Bessie was her own lovable self. "You're some sister! Ya havta enroll your own little sister in school today, and you're not even ready!"

"It's not me! It's my mother! She's saying goodbye to Deenie still! We're coming, we're coming!"

Deenie and I rushed down the stairs and caught up with the

stream of children heading toward Prince Arthur Street en route to Strathearn School.

"Ya know I want to be first in line!" Bessie continued to scold. And, to Deenie, "So *Mazal Tov*, Deenie. First time in school, eh? I hope ya get a good teacher, not a crank. My first teacher was just terrible. She made us sit stiff in class and ya couldn't go to the toilet. Only by recess. Yer glad yer going?"

But Deenie was too excited to speak or care. She skipped along happily, singing, "I'm going to school, my new shoes squeak."

Bessie overheard. "New shoes for school, eh? By us we get new shoes for *Yontif*," she referred to the High Holidays and Passover. "It's more important than for school."

We were all first generation Canadians. Yiddish was the language of our homes, with Russian or Polish used by our elders to convey information not for children's ears. Our first break with our parental ties were the English names given us by older siblings or teachers upon registration in the Protestant school. It was the baptism of anglicization where the names of saints, of Greek gods and goddesses, and of Anglo-Saxon heroes replaced the Jewish names given at birth to commemorate deceased parents or other relatives or friends. Thus *Chaya* (life) became Catherine, a good Catholic name, *Chaim* became Hyman (a Greek god), *Ita-Bayla* became Isabelle, *Yitschak* became Issie, Isadore, or Irving, and my Uncle *Laibi* became Lloyd. Thus my own name, *Shulamis*, honouring my maternal grandfather, *Shloime*, had become Sophie.

The thought of changing Deenie's name had never occurred to me. She had been named Dena Rochel for a great-aunt, and everyone called her Deenie.

"Waddaya gonna call her in school?" Bessie wanted to know.

"Deenie. Her name is Deenie. That's her name."

"They won't let. You'll see. You'll have to change it."

Bessie's brother Hymie interrupted our discussion. "Hey, Willie!" he shouted to a boy across the street, "Ya gonna be in my class?"

"Maybe," Willie shouted back. "Issie can't. He's not pimoded."

"Yeh, the teacher didn't like me!" Issie defended himself.

"Some teacher ya had!" Hymie abets. "A real…!"

"Don't say it!" Bessie interrupted from our side of the street. "If I tell Ma you called the teacher a dirty name, you'll get it."

Everyone walked along happily, dressed in his best for the occasion. Deeply implanted were the respect for learning, the magical hope for "a good beginning," and the desire to make a good impression on the new teacher and on friends.

"So waddlya call her?" Bessie asked again.

Deenie, completely euphoric, clung tightly to my hand as we marched along. In her off-tune little voice she sang the song she had made up on the spur of the moment,

Today is school, first day school,
My new shoes squeak, my new shoes squeak...

"Come faster," Bessie goaded again. "I told ya I wanna be first in line today!"

Strathearn School was located on Jeanne Mance above Prince Arthur, in the English neighbourhood on the west side of St. Lawrence Main. Prince Arthur was the street of little Jewish groceries and service stores, but Jeanne Mance wore an aura of elegance. Tall trees lined its sidewalks, and fine two-storey limestone dwellings with bay windows, little gardens, and long flights of outdoor wooden stairs with wrought-iron banisters marked it for good living. Up one flight, a little beyond the school, lived my last year's teacher, next door to where the Grade Three teacher who died from scarlet fever had lived. Around the block – this we only dared whisper to each other – lived the principal, and two streets east lived the "Office Teacher," the educational supervisor.

Strathearn School was new and beautiful. It was a four-storey brick building. Its bright classrooms with their large windows and freshly varnished desks invited learning. To most of us children it was the most splendid building we had ever seen.

Ninety-eight percent of the school population was Jewish and there were two Jewish teachers on the staff of thirty-five. Classes were co-educational but boys and girls congregated in separate basements with separate toilet facilities.

Deenie was impressed, no, thrilled. So thrilled that she immediately had to go to the toilet. Unaware of the facilities, she fretted.

"We have to go home. I have to make…"

"No." I smiled at her naïveté. "We go here."

She was delighted with the small toilets hidden in individual cubicles behind short wooden doors, with the roll of white toilet paper, unknown to her as it had been to all of us until we entered school, with the small sinks in which to wash our hands and with the roller towels to dry them. In a word, everything was new; everything delighted her. Even the feet beneath the stalls intrigued her.

"Look," she said. "Shoes. All kinds of shoes. Even big brown Oxfords like yours…" We smiled happily at each other and hand in hand returned to the basement to join my last year's line and await the bells.

Our principal was a fine gentleman of handsome bearing. He was soft-spoken, grandfatherly, and ran the school with discipline and decorum. Everyone feared, loved, and respected him. He took special delight in teaching us good manners and neatness. Just before bell-time, he appeared in the basement and moved quietly among the thronging children, slowing them down, pointing with his cane to a piece of paper or a bit of orange peel on the floor and to the large metal garbage bin. A nod from him was a command. Thanks to the standards he set, and to our ever-sweeping caretaker, our basement and school were always tidy despite the hundreds of children who milled there all day.

With the first bell there appeared at the head of the stairs a drummer boy in Boy Scout attire, drum and sticks at attention. With the second bell, the children moved into their respective classroom groups, in columns, two by two, led by the Grade Seven girls who were supposed to set an example. The third bell signalled the drummer to beat an advance and, proudly and rhythmically, we marched silently upstairs to our various rooms to the spirited rat-a-tat of the drum. The mood was broken only by the authoritative voice of monitors who called out at intervals, "Stop whispering in line or I take you to the office!"

Happily dragging my bedazzled Deenie by the hand, I reached the door of my classroom.

"Please, Miss," I addressed my teacher, "This is my little sister

Deenie. I have to write her in today."

"You have to what?" she asked in genteel tones.

"I have to write her in. I mean *enroll* her. She needs to go to kindergarten."

"You mean you want to register her. You may take her to the office."

At the office, a long line of children was waiting to be registered. They waited with parents or with older siblings. We joined them. "Let's wait here by the lockers," I directed. "You have to stand on the white line with your toes together."

We waited.

The office teacher, Miss Bradshaw, sat at her desk "writing in" the new children. The lady before us had brought a little boy from Scotland. His name was Donald MacGlashen. Miss Bradshaw smiled, greeted the mother graciously, and commented, "From the Auld Country. How nice! Donald will do well here. We're glad to have him." She proceeded with the registration.

"And who is this?" she asked me as Mrs. MacGlashen left.

"It's my sister Deenie," I pushed Deenie forward with pride.

"What's your name, little girl?" she addressed Deenie.

"I'm Deenie."

"Jeanie?"

"No. Deenie. Deenie Borodensky. My father and mother come from the Old Country too," Deenie offered her credentials. Miss Bradshaw smiled. Suddenly she seemed to have something in her left eye – an unseen speck that she tried to wipe out as her right hand covered her face. "Really? How nice. What is your name in English?" Deenie turned to me. I froze. What other name could Deenie have?

"Her English name," Miss Bradshaw repeated, turning to me.

Suddenly I was inspired. At the Globe Theatre on Saturday afternoon we had cried ourselves sick over *Orphans of the Storm*! Oh, those poor little sisters, those brave little outcasts – Lillian and Dorothy Gish! How beautifully they had suffered! Lillian and *Dorothy* Gish. Heaven is my witness – her name began with a D!

"Her name is Dorothy," I announced proudly, "Dorothy, like by Lillian and Dorothy Gish…"

"Dorothy?" Miss Bradshaw smiled, "And are you from the Old

Country too?"

"No. I'm Deenie from Coloniale Avenue," she answered bravely.

"And you want to go to kindergarten?" Miss Bradshaw really liked Deenie.

Deenie beamed, "Yes."

"Then come with me Dorothy," said Miss Bradshaw, gently taking Deenie by the hand. "We'll go together. You may return to your classroom," she nodded to me.

And without so much as a wave of farewell, Deenie, now Dorothy, disappeared down the long darkening corridor into the new world of Canadian English culture.

~

[This following diary entry exemplifies a recurring theme with Shulamis. She never felt a secure sense of belonging. She had learned, as a little girl in her Bubbie's home, that becoming a performer was the only way she could attract full attention in the busy household where she competed with the complicated lives of her many aunts and uncles. From a very early age, she conceived, wrote, and read her stories and recited her poetry to a growing audience. She continued to garner praise as a gifted performer throughout her life. While her talent brought her acceptance and admiration, it did not necessarily bring her the love that she craved. In her later years, the abrupt descent from euphoria during her presentations to the crashing depression after was always devastating. Shulamis often phoned Gilah at the lowest of these times. Mother and daughter were able to speak cogently about this psychological difficulty; Gilah would suggest to her mother that if only she could bottle limelight, she would daily anoint Shulamis with that radiant elixir to repel the inevitable crash. Even in her most desperate moments, Shulamis was able to perceive both the humour and the relevance of this image. Although initially grateful for the compassionate ear, her inability to control her resentment often grew to rage, and she would lash out fiercely against her daughter.]

∿ Diary entry June 11, 1974

I remember the first time I really felt a moment of belonging: Grade IV Xmas. The girls asked me to be in a play with them. I was to be the maid. But I loved it. We had no script – just a general idea. It started well, but then went wild and while I was in it, I remember feeling hilariously happy, – but it ran amok & I began to feel silly & ran out.

∿

WINNIE GOES HOME

ANOTHER YEAR HAD COME and gone; another summer had passed. The new school term and the oncoming High Holidays absorbed our attention. Mamma and Winnie had stripped the summer throws off the furniture. Winnie had rolled the rugs onto the floors again. The freshly washed curtains lit up the rooms and the icebox and pantry were newly scrubbed and filled with the bounty of the harvest to greet the New Year. We children were delighted to find our friends again. With school and the after-school Jewish classes, we spent few waking hours at home.

Winnie was now part of our family. She worked, served, and moved in and about our lives. But something about her had changed. She was no longer the loud, laughing, prank-playing country bump-kin we had known. Even Deenie noticed it.

"Something is different with Winnie," I said to her one day.

"Yeh. She doesn't laugh like in the country... What's the matter with her?"

"Maybe she's sick. Let's try to make her laugh."

"Winnie, make like a bat," I urged at supper, putting my hands to my temples and wagging my fingers as she had done. Winnie only turned and walked out of the room and I heard the lock turn in the bathroom. I was asleep when she came into the bedroom, and even in my sleep I thought I could hear Winnie weeping.

Mamma, too, was perturbed.

"I don't know what's happened to her," I heard her say to Papa one day, "She's not the same at all since we're at home."

"Maybe she misses her friends in the country. Maybe she's in love," Papa replied.

"Maybe I should talk to her..." Mamma said. But when Mamma asked Winnie if anything was wrong, Winnie said no, and went about her work.

Auntie was the one to see the obvious. "Vichna," she said one day to Mamma, "Your girl is pregnant."

"You're mad!" Mamma exploded, "You and your ideas!"

"I'm telling you she's pregnant," Auntie insisted. "Look at her breasts."

"And if she is, what can we do about it?" asked Papa.

What sort of talk is this?" I wondered. "Papa, Winnie isn't even married!" I said. "How can she be pregnant?"

"Right," said Papa, patting my back as I stood before him. "Just don't give it another thought. Have you finished your homework?"

I nodded.

"Then go to bed like a good girl. Good night, dear."

As the weeks went on, I watched Winnie with ever-growing wonder and concern. Several times, when I came in unannounced, conversation between her and Mamma came to a sudden halt. Often during the night I heard Winnie weeping, but I didn't dare move lest I disturb her even more. She certainly wasn't eating as much at mealtimes, yet she was certainly getting fatter.

Chanukah and Christmas were approaching. There would be holidays from school and festivities at home. Winnie, who on her arrival had stipulated that she must have the right to go home for Christmas, now made no mention of claiming that right.

"I want to see how you celebrate the holidays," she said when I asked her.

We lit the Chanukah candles those eight nights and received little bags with Chanukah money from Papa. Winnie got her little bag too, but she stood sadly, nodded her head and said nothing. As Christmas drew nearer she began to make Christmas stockings for Deenie and me. Mamma was distressed.

"Christmas stockings in a Jewish house? Crazy!" she remonstrated to Papa.

"Let her. She's unhappy. The children know it's not their holiday." There was no laughter in Winnie.

"How much longer do you intend to keep her?" I heard my Auntie ask Mamma one snowy afternoon as they were sipping the tea that Winnie had served them in the dining room. I was in the kitchen getting my milk and bread and jam before going to my Jewish classes.

"I don't know. She has nowhere to go. She doesn't want her family to know. I don't know what to do."

"Has she seen a doctor?"

"I took her to the clinic at the hospital last week. They say she's fine."

"What about the father?"

"They asked her. She refuses to say anything about him. I asked her too."

"So what will she do with the baby? She can't keep it!"

"The Social Services said she should give it to the nuns."

"So what did she say?"

"She began to cry. I must tell you – I cried too," said Mamma.

The glass fell from my hand with a clatter. Then it was true! Winnie wasn't married and she was going to have a baby! And they were telling her to give the baby away!

"What's happening there?" Mamma called to me. "Better be more careful."

I didn't know whether to weep or rejoice for Winnie. She was having a baby! How wonderful! But she would have to give it away! And how could a baby have no father? It was clear I wasn't to ask about that at home.

As usual, Bessie was my source of information. As we filed out at noon to get our coats from the lockers, I called to her, "Bessie, walk home with me lunchtime. I have to tell you something."

We shuffled through the snowbanks on Prince Arthur Street but I couldn't bring myself to talk about Winnie. Bessie was soon impatient.

"So? Tell me already. What's the secret?"

"Bessie – our maid Winnie – she's got a baby…"

"Yeh? So *Mazal Tov*! When did she get it? Boy or girl?"

"We don't know yet. It's still inside."

"Yeh? So where's her husband? He lives by you too?"

"No. She doesn't have a husband. She just got a baby."

Bessie stopped suddenly, one leg suspended. "Ya mean she fucked a boy and got pregning? Oy vay! When?"

"Naw Bessie! Not like that! She's just very fat – and I heard my mother tell my Auntie that the hospital wants…"

"What d'ya mean, 'Not like that'? It's the only way! Ya donno how ya get a baby? Ya fuck so ya get!"

"No, Bessie! Not our Winnie!" Everything in me was crying, "Not like that! That's dirty!" But to Bessie I said, "Stop it, Bessie. It's Winnie's baby. It's her own baby!"

"She must of got it in the country. Them farmer Frenchies – they get lots of babies – always. Boys. Girls. Whole gangs. Hmmmm."

"Bessie, I – I wish we could keep that baby in our house."

"Ya crazy!" she blared. "A *mumzer* (bastard)! Jews don't like *mumzers*. My mother would throw her down the stairs!"

I ached for Winnie and her baby and spent restless nights worrying about them. Spring had begun to show itself and Winnie was very, very big. I heard Mamma say to Papa, "I'll have to get a woman in to wash the walls down for Passover." But Winnie wouldn't hear of it. One Tuesday afternoon, when Mamma went out, Winnie got the ladder and washed the dining room walls. Mamma was horrified when she came in and caught her finishing the job.

"Winnie! It's not for you! I'll get someone else to do it!"

"I do my job, Madame," she said and burst out crying. "You so good for me!"

One April night, just before Passover, Winnie woke suddenly with a moan.

"Winnie, what's wrong?" I asked.

"Dat alright. You sleep," she said softly, beginning to get dressed. She pulled a small valise from under her bed and went out of the room. I heard her muffled voice on the phone and then heard the door shut.

Next morning, Mamma greeted me at breakfast.

"Winnie had a baby. A boy. They just phoned from the hospital."

I trembled. "Mamma, can we see it – the baby?"

"No. You go to school. I'll go visit her this afternoon and tell you about it after school."

Mamma visited Winnie every day at the Hôpital Française, later Hôpital Jeanne d'Arc. She never went empty-handed. One evening she said to us, "I have good news. Winnie's baby is going home today – to a very good home. No, not to Winnie's home, but to a nice family that has no children of their own."

"And Winnie?" I asked, my eyes full of tears.

"And Winnie is going back to her parents' home for a while. One day she will marry and have other babies of her own."

"But why can't she stay by us?" I pleaded.

"I asked her, but she said she wants to go home."

We all went to see Winnie off. As we stood at the CPR station Deenie and I were crying. Mamma was biting her lip. Papa gave Winnie a big box of chocolates "for the road" and carried her luggage onto the train. He seated Winnie at a window.

Winnie was weeping as she waved to us from the open window. "I never forget you!" She cried. "Never! Never!"

"Come back to us, Winnie," I called. "I'll never forget you too…!"

∾

SHEKSPIR WAS JEWIS

THE ROAD HOME from Strathearn School seemed longer than usual that dull November afternoon. It was already after four o'clock and Mamma would be worried. But not half so worried as when I would tell her what had happened in school that afternoon.

No need to ask if Mamma was at home. Mamma had to rest a lot and we had to be good children and not aggravate her.

As I turned the doorknob I heard her voice.

"So late you're from school?"

"I had to help the teacher correct spelling books." Mamma and I considered this an honour.

"Nice," said Mamma. "You going to *Shule* now?"

"Yes, Mamma. But first I have to do my homework for *Lereren* Sherr."

"First eat something," Mamma offered. "The bread man brought fresh *kimmel* bread. Don't forget to shake up the milk or you'll take off all the cream."

"Don't worry Mamma. I'll do it."

I entered the dining room and laid my books on the massive oak table. I was not at ease.

It was hard to stay after school with such turmoil in my heart, even to help the teacher. Now I had to hurry or I'd be late.

As I bit into the great buttered oval of crusty bread fragrant with Mamma's luscious plum jam, I was tense. Surely I couldn't break this news to Mamma. If only it had happened in the morning. Then I would have discussed it with Papa when he came home for lunch; but it had happened in the afternoon, and he worked late every night in his tailor shop on Main Street.

The sideboard facing me held the secret of my distress. It was made of polished oak, like the round table and high-backed leather-seated chairs, its lower section a china cabinet with brass-knobbed leaded glass doors. Instead of holding our new set of porcelain dishes, our china cabinet held books. Papa, a self-taught man, loved books, and just as Mamma saved her pennies to pay Mr. Popper, the peddler, fifty cents a week until the china was paid for, Papa spent his pin-money on books. The books stood in two rows, one behind the other, in their colourful cloth bindings, some singly, others in sets of two or more. The newest acquisitions always had the place of honour up front.

"Books are teachers," Papa said, "and you have to give them a place of honour in your home."

Thus it was that I first became acquainted with the names of Tolstoy, Pushkin, Chekhov, Dostoievsky, and with our own Yiddish classicists: Mendele, Peretz, Sholem Aleichem and – Shekspir.

The gold letters on the red cloth binding announced proudly in Yiddish: *Shylock – Der Koifman fun Venedig* (Shylock, the Merchant of Venice) … *fun Villiam Shekspir*. How was I to know that Shakespeare wasn't a Jew? Had I ever heard his name anywhere else than at home or in any language other than Yiddish?

So when our Grade Four teacher told us that afternoon in the English public school that she was going to read us "a tale from Shakespeare," I raised my hand.

"Please, Miss, we have him at home in the china cabinet."

"In the china cabinet?" she had repeated in amazement, her lovely British accent trailing into the halls of Strathearn School. "What? – I mean whom?"

"Shekspir!" I announced proudly.

"Do your parents read English?" she asked with interest.

"They don't have to. Shekspir writes in Yiddish. He's Jewish so he writes in Yiddish."

Miss Cranshaw was aghast.

"Who told you this?" she asked.

"Nobody." I was mistress of the situation. "My father buys his books. We keep him in our new china cabinet where we keep all the books."

"In Yiddish?" Miss Cranshaw asked again. "You're sure it's Shakespeare?"

"Sure I'm sure! The book is about Shylock, a Jew who . . ."

"Of course!" Miss Cranshaw was relieved. "Shakespeare did write a book about a Jew called Shylock. But Shakespeare was an Englishman – perhaps the greatest Englishman who ever lived. And he wrote in English, more than 300 years ago, in beautiful poetry. In English!"

The children laughed. All but three of the thirty-six were Jews. They became self-conscious. They laughed.

My eyes filled with tears. What was going on here? Why were they laughing? Surely they knew I was telling the truth!

"The whole book is in Yiddish!" I insisted.

"Well, Shylock was hardly a Jew to be proud of," said Miss Cranshaw coldly. "Why would your father want that book on his shelf?"

How could I break this news to Mamma? What could I tell her? If only Papa had been at home!

As I struggled with my Yiddish homework, I decided to spare her. I'd speak to my Jewish teacher. Surely she'd help me right this slander!

I ran all the way to *Shule*. I caught my teacher just as she was about to enter the classroom.

"*Lereren* Sherr," I gasped in Yiddish, "I must ask you something."

"Yes, Shulamis?" She called me by my Jewish name.

"I told my teacher in school today that Shekspir is Jewish and he writes in Yiddish."

Lereren Sherr's pretty face suggested a smile.

"She says he is not a Jew! She says he's an Englishman and he lived more than 300 years ago!" I trembled with indignation.

Miss Sherr put her arm around my shoulder.

"Don't cry!" she consoled me softly. "William Shakespeare *was* an Englishman." She spoke his name as it is spoken in English. "And he did write in English more than 300 years ago."

"So why is he in our china cabinet in Yiddish?" I pleaded.

"Because Shakespeare was a great man with a great heart and a great talent," she answered gently. "He now belongs to the whole world. We read him in Yiddish because he is translated into Yiddish. And into many other languages. Because Jews and other people want to know what Shakespeare has to say."

"And Shylock – what's wrong with Shylock?" I sobbed. "She says we can't be proud of Shylock and my father shouldn't keep him on the shelf!"

"Come into the classroom, Shulamis. Come. We will talk about it in class." She ushered me through the open door.

Slowly, slowly the world spread out before me, and it would be a long time before I felt at home in the world outside my father's house.

∞ Diary entry - July 2, 1975

Papa is great. Looks beautiful in his new grey suit.

When I gave him my book [*Seeded in Sinai*], I showed him the dictionary he had given me in 1928 with the inscription: *Dizen buch gib ich mein tochter zi zol gefinen verter ir helfen in ir gestoker arbet.* [Trans: This book I give to my daughter that she may find words to help her with her distinguished work.]

"Papa, this is the answer to your blessing." I'm glad we both lived to see it.

∼

DEENIE NEEDS A TONIC

THE DINING-ROOM CLOCK read 8:15. We had to leave for school. It was winter, and our Deenie, who had just recovered from another cold, would return to school this morning after an absence of a whole week. I was a robust girl of ten. Deenie was six; a pale, thin little girl, prone to nose colds, sore throat and ears.

Our mother had spoken to Mr. Schmerling, the druggist, who decided Deenie needed a tonic. He especially recommended Scott's Emulsion, a fine blend of cod liver oil and other good things, a tried and true remedy against the Canadian winter's blast.

The great bottle of white, thick, greasy fluid stood on the buffet of the china cabinet in full view, and every morning after breakfast the war was on.

Mamma fired the first shot.

"*Dinyela*," she used the diminutive, "take the molshon."

Deenie was a child of few words.

"No," she said, turning to get her street clothes from the rack in the hall.

"*Dinyela, Tochter*," Mamma repeated more persuasively from the doorway, "take the *molshon*."

"No," repeated Deenie, leaning against the door with her right rubber in her hands.

"It's so good – it smells like ice cream..." pleaded Mamma.

"It's slippery and it stinks offish!" retorted Deenie, shuddering.

"*Dinyela, Tochter*," pleaded Mamma again, carrying the heavy Russian tablespoon of white sticky stuff into the hall. "Take the molshon so you won't be green and skinny. Do like Mr. Schmerling says so you'll get healthy and strong!"

Deenie didn't even raise her voice.

"I just said I won't take it!" She pulled her crocheted tam over her sensitive ears to keep Mamma out.

"*Gottinyu!*" Mamma called to God for reinforcements, "What shall I do with this child? Pale and skinny like a toothpick, and so cold outside you could catch nyemonya, and you won't even hear!"

"Mamma, we'll be late for school," I interceded. Addressing Deenie by her public school name to remind her of the obedience it implied, I added, "Dorothy, take the molshon! We'll be late for school. Hurry already!"

Deenie was becoming impatient too. Hugging her winter coat tightly to her, she suddenly howled, "I said I won't take it! It stinks fish!"

Mamma was beside herself.

"Woe is me! Like this you speak to a mother? Like this you speak of a healthy medicine? Shame on you! Me? If the doctor told me I should eat (you should excuse me) *you know what*, I would eat it to become strong and healthy!"

"Take the cod liver oil, Deenie," I pressed again, louder this time. "Take it! Don't be such a baby! Let's go to school already!"

"A dollar and a half a bottle," wailed Mamma, "and she won't take it! What shall I do with it? Throw it out?"

Heaven forbid. In our house nothing that was possibly useful was thrown out. You never knew when you might need it. As for food, "It's a sin to throw out good food. So many poor children in Russia would lick their fingers . . ." This last statement I expected to see any day – in Mamma's red Russian cross-stitch – on our kitchen wall.

Deenie had no sympathy for the poor children in Russia. She ate what she liked and left the rest.

My conscience was clear. I ate everything. And I looked it.

Silence hung heavy on the air, broken only by the sound of Deenie kicking the door with her right rubber-covered shoe. The clock struck 8:30. I pictured the principal, Mr. Kneeland, moving about in the school basement where the lines formed to march upstairs.

"Deenie Borodensky! Take it!" I cried. "We'll be late for lines! We'll have to go to the office!"

Deenie was now in tears.

"Lemme alone! I don't care!" And sobbing, "I'll never take it in my whole, whole life!"

Philip and Vichna in their apartment on Hutchison Street.
Jewish Public Library.

Mamma finally got the message.

"Stubborn like a Borodensky *Kohen*!" she exploded, evoking the stubbornness of Papa and his brethren, descendants of the ancient Temple priests, who were blemished with this trait. "*Nu*, so what shall we do with the molshon?"

Suddenly she turned to me.

"Sophela, *Tochter* – you're a big girl. She's a baby. It's a shame to throw out such a healthy molshon! A dollar and a half a bottle! You take it, *Tochter*. You show her…"

"Mamma, no!" I cried. "I'm not skinny! I don't get colds!"

"Think of the poor children in Russia!" Mamma pleaded. "Such a pity on them! You mustn't waste. *Who lives without account dies without a shroud*!"

Mamma's proverbs struck horror in my heart.

"Mamma, don't! I'll take it! I won't let it go to waste!" I clenched my fists and held my breath as the great tablespoon went between my teeth. As I swallowed, shuddering with distaste, Deenie opened the door to the street and I heard her twitter in her little-girl voice: "It's healthy! It tastes like vanilla ice cream. Mr. Schmerling says it's good . . ."

℘ Diary excerpt [undated]

My Birthday Party
For my eleventh birthday Mamma said I could have a party.

I invited 8 children (2) from my class, (6) from the street (sic). They came. Some brought presents.

Mamma sat us around the oak dining table & gave each child a bottle of "ginger ale" & a piece of cake. There was no joy at the table, no bday cake, no singing <u>Happy Bday</u>, no games. Mamma had done her part. I had begged and pleaded to have a party. I can still see her strained white face beneath her mass of wavy auburn hair, her long neck reaching out of her white blouse as she bent to serve each child.

The children drank their ginger ale, ate their cake & went home.

The next day none spoke to me. Only one – who came to the house to ask to have her present returned, a gold-coloured mechanical pencil with which I had begun to write & which I had cherished.

"My sister said you should give me back my present. That was some rotten party!"

Mamma said to give back the gift & comforted me that it didn't matter but I felt all the lonelier after that.

∽

THE GIRL WHO STOLE SANTA CLAUS

Chanukah had just passed and it was Monday morning. We had celebrated at home with candles, latkes, and Chanukah *gelt* for which Papa had made us special little white-and-blue striped cotton bags. The festivities at *Shule* – the decorations, the story-telling, the songs, and the special concert – all had been topped off by the celebration at my Bubbie's house the night before. My ears still rang with the shouts of pleasure as family and friends greeted each other, with Zaida's voice chanting the blessings over the full menorah, the flames of its nine small coloured candles dancing out the Miracle of the Oil. My tongue still tingled with the taste of the fine, hot, yeast-blown pancakes dripping with goose fat and brown molten honey kept warm in a large basin at the edge of the stove.

I licked my lips in pleasant memory as I clutched my little bag of coins we children had been encouraged to collect from the adults. This was Chanukah *gelt*, commemorating the coin Judah the Maccabee had struck to mark the victory over the Greeks and the rededication of the Temple.

Suddenly I realized there were no children on the street. Again I was late for school? I began to run, the blurred edges of the Temple receding into the realities of Prince Arthur Street leading to Strathearn School.

As I charged up the stairs to my classroom, I tucked my private world into my heart, took my seat, and readied myself for the dichotomy that ordered our lives.

After the recital of the Lord's Prayer that everyone, except Bessie, repeated in unison, Miss Cranshaw handed out an arithmetic assignment and we, the five scripture takers, went to our accustomed corner in back of the room for our private rendezvous with "the Lord." Christmas was two weeks away and at Strathearn School the windows were blooming with red and green bells, Santas and winter scenes. Our class was making little calendars, Christmas gifts for our parents.

Miss Cranshaw opened her Bible and read:

And there were in the same country shepherds abiding in the fields keeping watch over their flocks by night. And the Angel

of the Lord came upon them and the glory of the Lord shone
around about them and they were sore afraid. And the Angel
said unto them, "Fear not, for I bring you good tidings of great
joy which shall be unto all people. For unto you is born this day
in the city of David, a Saviour which is Christ the Lord."

And together with the three Christian children and Annie, "the scholarship girl," I listened carefully to the beautiful melodious rhythms of the King James version of the New Testament, the words inscribing themselves indelibly in my memory. I listened. I enjoyed. Yet somehow a shrill note was struck within me: The City of David I knew; the Angel of the Lord I recognized. But – the Saviour which is Christ? Christ the Lord? Unless – unless, of course, God and the Lord were not quite the same . . .

"They could have their Lord!" Bessie barked when I told my friends about it at recess.

"I wish we could have Christmas," mourned Sarah. "It's so pretty with a Christmas tree. You saw by Malo's candy store the Christmas tree they put up? And so beautiful decorated with silver streamers and snow and on top with aangel. . ."

"That's their 'angel of the Lord,'" hissed Bessie. "Ya know, ya should-n't even go there now. My mother makes me peanut briddle at home."

I was much disturbed by the Christmas tree at Malo's. It was beautiful and magical, but somewhere in my head there was a fence with a sign on it that read:

Malo's Candy Store corner Cadieux and Prince Arthur is good
for candy and scribblers and things, but that's all.

Three women kept the store: tall, sad-eyed, pretty women, a mother and two fading daughters; they spoke only French. They lived on Colonial Avenue near us, behind wooden double doors and blind-drawn windows in the self-contained cottage next to the lane. One rarely saw any movement in or out of those doors. I clearly recall the black crepe and the wreath that had decorated those doors the previous winter as through the silent snow had run the news that Mr. Malo was dead. He had never served us, but I remember him showing himself occasionally from behind the shiny green curtains at the back of the store. That summer and every summer after that, there bloomed a tiny garden in front of their house a pretty bush of bleeding hearts, so beautiful, so sad.

After his death, the three ladies – dressed in black with a white lace ruffle at the neck – continued to run the store themselves. No matter how noisy the children were on the street, when we entered Malo's we dropped our voices, and while we took our time choosing and deciding on which best buy to spend our two cents, we spoke politely.

Sarah lived on Cadieux Street (now de Bullion), across from Malo's.

When we met after lunch to return together to school, Sarah was again full of the Christmas tree at Malo's.

"They have little white furry Santa Clauses on it too, now, and they were just putting on candles when I was there!" she exulted. "You should see how beautiful it is! I just *wish* we could have a Christmas tree!"

"What are you saying? We just had Chanukah!" I tried to ease her.

"Sure! But what's Chanukah? My mother made me a few latkes and she gave me some Chanukah *gelt* – a quarter – so?"

"Didn't your father light the candles?" I asked again. "And didn't they tell you about the oil – how it burned eight days instead of one? And about the brave Maccabees, how Mattathias yelled, 'Who is for the Lord follow me!' And his son Judah, the Hammer, freed the Jews from the Greeks . . ." I grew increasingly more excited as I relived the pleasure of the week.

"Sophie, I'm not like you. I don't go to *Shule* and I don't have a Bubbie here. And my father didn't tell me nothing. He works late in the dress factory – and they don't believe in it!"

"They don't?" I was distressed.

"They're *narkistin* (Anarchists)," she defended.

"What's *narkistin*?" I asked.

"I don't know but I know it's good. They want everybody should be good and should be free – everybody. But it's not with God and it's not with holidays . . ."

"So how do they have fun?" I persisted.

"They talk. They have friends and they come to our house and they make speeches and they talk. They have a lady comes sometimes from New York and her name is Emma Goldman.

"She talks loud and tells them they have to make the world free. Then they sing songs and have tea with lemon and sponge cake."

"They didn't tell you about the Maccabees?" I asked again.

Something terrible was happening to the gentle Sarah.

"No," she replied. "My parents want all people should be free and make a good world. Not just Jews. They don't like *no* religion."

Preparations for Christmas took over. Because of fear of possible fire, we had no class tree, but Miss Cranshaw had set up a crèche on the book table at the front of the room. It was made of cardboard and it was painted red and green and had white sparkling snow for a ground. In the centre stood a tiny cradle with the Christ Child in it, a shining halo carefully attached to his pretty head, and Mary and Joseph and the Wise Men knelt before Him. On the backdrop oxen and sheep were painted. We sang "Silent Night" and "Away in a Manger" and "Good King Wenceslas" and I rejoiced in the beautiful music as the words drifted into the hall to join with the voices of the other classes, composed largely of Jewish children, who were also preparing for Christmas and looking forward to the holiday that would follow.

On Tuesday Sarah brought a ball to school and at recess we played Stando in the basement. We looked ahead to the winter break when we would be free for ten whole days to play outside and go skating and sliding in St. Louis Square.

Three or four days before the holidays, Miss Cranshaw looked up at Sarah and said, "Why so pale, Sarah? You look like you had fallen into a flour barrel." Sarah did not answer. She lowered her eyes and covered her face with her hands. Next day, and until classes broke for the holidays, Sarah did not appear in school. I was sorry she was missing the excitement of the season. Only Bessie couldn't allow herself to enjoy the scene. "Good she's not here. She doesn't have to be here. Every day, 'holy, holy'! It's enough already."

On my way home from our Christmas party, I rang Sarah's bell. Her mother answered.

"How is Sarah?"

"She's better now. She had a very high fever."

"Tonsils?" I asked again.

"No, the doctor didn't know what it was. But today she is better. No, don't come in. In a day or two she'll come out to play."

"I brought her the calendar she made in school and the teacher sent her candy, like we all got."

"Thank you, Sophie. I'll give it to her. Thank you."

Every morning when I went out to play I walked by Sarah's house to see if she was out. It was only towards the end of the week that I found her sitting at the top of her stairs, huddled in her heavy coat and scarf. She was even paler than I remembered her in school that day. She was feeding the birds bits of white bread.

When she saw me she tried to turn away.

"Sarah," I called softly from the foot of the iron staircase.

She rose, sending the two sparrows on the banister into flight.

"Sarah, how are you feeling?" I tried again.

"I—I'm a little better," she answered looking away.

"May I come up and talk to you?"

"Come – but I don't feel good." And suddenly she was weeping into her mittens.

I ran up the stairs. "What hurts you, Sarah?" I wanted to cry too.

"In here." She put her hand on the left side of her chest, then bent over and continued to weep.

"What does the doctor say?"

"He says nothing. What does the doctor know! He just gives bitter medicines. And now he says I should go play outside."

"So take your red ball and we'll play."

"I don't have my red ball any more." She looked up at me and suddenly again broke into tears. "I threw it away."

"Sarah, why? Why did you throw away such a good red ball?"

"It made me sick!" She sobbed. "That rotten ball! It's all on account of that rotten ball!"

I squatted beside her on the stair, and put my arm around her. "Sarahla," I pleaded, "Everybody catches a cold sometimes. So what?"

"No, Sophie. It wasn't just a cold. It wasn't a cold at all."

We sat together for what seemed hours as Sarah tried to control her weeping. Finally she looked up. "Sophie, swear. Swear you should drop down dead if you tell anyone!" her frightened red eyes looked into mine.

"I should – I should drop down dead!" I uttered, horrified at the thought.

"Swear 'Two fingers up to God'," she looked at me threateningly.

"Two fingers up to God!" I repeated in horror, pulling off my right mitten and raising the first two fingers of my right hand to the sky.

"Nobody, you hear? You shouldn't tell nobody! Speshly that – that Bessie! You hear? Even not your own mother! It's a suchy terrible secret!" She was sobbing again.

Then it poured out.

On the first day of Chanukah, Sarah's mother had given her Chanukah *gelt*: two new silver dimes and a tiny silver nickel. Sarah had played alone with the money before she went to sleep. She had hoarded it all week as she listened to the other children tell how much they had received from aunts and uncles. With no relatives who celebrated the holiday, Sarah's hoard had not grown.

Each day as she went into Malo's for her two cents' worth of candy, she peered around, wondering what she might buy for her precious twenty-five cents. As the excitement over Christmas grew in the school, Sarah decided she would buy that twenty-five cent red rubber ball. Then she could play with the other children and everyone would see how great her Chanukah *gelt* really was.

I had gone with her to buy the ball.

"Try it," I urged when she paid her money. "Try it. See how high it jumps!"

Sarah was bouncing the ball when Madame Malo suddenly spoke up in a loud, clear voice. "Outside!" she ordered.

Sarah was caught unawares. The ball suddenly jumped to unexpected heights and before she could catch it, it bounced on the counter and fell on the floor behind the counter. Madame Malo, who had already moved to the centre of the floor, looked at her severely and said, "Tiens, get it – get it!"

Sarah went into the magic land behind the counter. Lots of boxes were stacked high upon each other. At the top of the stacks – she could not believe her own eyes – lay two open boxes full of little white furry Santa Clauses, the same as adorned the Malo's Christmas tree! The temptation was too great. Sarah grabbed a handful – two Santas to be exact – and pushed them into the top of her long red woolen overstocking. Madame Malo's impatient voice rose from the side of the store.

"Eh bien, tu as la balle?"

Sarah picked up her ball, and with a panicky look, came around the counter. As we walked to school, I said, "Sarah, why are you so red? You didn't do nothing wrong. She told you to go get the ball."

Sarah began to run. I ran after her. "Sarah! Sarah! Wait for me!" But Sarah did not stop until she got to the school basement. The next day, Miss Cranshaw noticed her pallor.

"And I couldn't sleep no more!" wailed poor Sarah, finishing her terrible confession. "I just couldn't sleep at all! Then I began to feel so hot! My mother took my temperature and it was burning! Once I slept and I dreamt she was chasing me, Madame Malo, and yelling, 'Police! Police! Dis terrible girl – she stoled Santy Claus!' In English yet! Everybody from school was shouting, 'Shame! Shame! Christmas, and she stole Santa Claus!'"

I was too stunned to speak. I sat looking at her, rigid like the icicle that hung from the balcony above.

"Poor Sarah!" I finally uttered.

"Don't 'poor' me!" She jumped up in fury. "It's your fault too! Don't be so innocent! You with your Chanukah, and your family, and your *Shule*! Every day a new story about how much fun you had. And the school with the Christmas and the Baby Jesus! I'm Jewish and what do I have? Nothing! A rotten red rubber ball!"

I was terrified that her mother might open the door and hear what was going on. That I should be a partner to the crime had never even entered my mind! What could I tell her? How could I comfort her?

Suddenly I had an idea. "Sarah, you know, you could go to *Shule* too. You don't even have to pay if you can't afford. I'm telling you. Talk to your mother . . ."

Sarah clutched my arm. "You swore! You swore to God you won't tell!" she panicked.

"I won't. I promise. I swear again. I just said you should talk to your mother she should write you in in *Shule.* In Peretz Shule it's not so much with God, but it's with stories and songs and holidays. We could go together . . ." She looked at me eagerly. Encouraged, I continued, "The teacher could call you Soreh like she calls me Shulamis. Then you could have everything too . . ."

There was a long moment of silence; then Sarah rose and rubbed her eyes with her heavy coat sleeve. We stood looking at each other.

"I have to go in now," she said turning from me.

"You'll tell your mother about *Shule*?" I pressed again.

"Yes, Sophie, I'll try."

"Soreh," I offered, unwilling to let her go, "You could call me by my Jewish name, Shulamis."

Sarah smiled gratefully. "Thank you, Shulamis."

"Goodbye, Soreh," I kissed her quickly on the cheek and ran down the stairs.

~

THE JOYS OF WINTER

"I HATE THEM! I hate them! I'm not gonna wear them! They itch!" I shouted.

The season had arrived and with it, the long woolen underwear called "*Vesh*," to protect us from the harsh Canadian winter.

"And see how my feet look!" I continued to wail. "Like elephants! I can't make my stockings look nice in my boots with the *vesh* inside!"

"Yeh, and it's hard to go to the toilet with buttons in the back," my little sister Deenie added. "It takes so long! Yesterday, I nearly . . ."

Mamma was strong on sense. "It's cold outside. Winter you have to dress warm, not fancy."

"I'll better be cold!" I wailed again. "I'm not gonna wear them! Mamma, I'm in Grade Six already. I'm not in baby class! Some of

106

the girls wear brazeers already!"

Mamma was adamant. "In winter you have to dress warm, not fancy."

"So we have high-lace boots and overstockings and rubbers and sweaters and winter coats . . ."

"Yeh, and crocheted hats and long scarves and mitts and the little camphor *zekela*" Deenie enumerated, fingering at her neck the cotton camphor bag Mamma had hand-sewn for her.

"That's right," Mamma agreed. "That's right. Don't forget the camphor *zekela*. Comes the winter comes the flu."

Oh, the Canadian winter! The snowbanks on Coloniale Avenue were so high you couldn't see across to the other side of the street. Horses pulled sleighs down the middle, blazing paths that steamed with hot manure, decorated with clusters of sparrows enjoying feast in famine. Snow forts and snowballs abounded. Teams shaped up: boys against girls, one side of the street against the other, this gang against that. Only skating broke down the barriers as we all planned to go to the skating rink at Fletcher's Field to inaugurate the season.

At home, every day brought its crisis. Yesterday it was the *vesh*, today it is the skating suit. Papa had made me a pair of knickers, grey English wool with brown check, but I needed a skating sweater.

"Mamma," I pleaded for the ninth time, "Mamma, I need a skating sweater."

"For Chanukah you'll get a skating suit," Mamma announced.

A heavy snow had fallen. Chanukah was still a whole week away. Since Tuesday I had been wondering about the great cardboard box in the hall closet.

"Mamma, what's the big box in the hall cupboard?"

Mamma teaches patience. "A person has to learn to wait," she replied. "A person has to learn patience. You'll see when it's time . . ."

"When, Mamma?"

"Later."

"When later?"

"Chanukah."

So I waited.

The first night of Chanukah fell on Thursday. I rushed into the house after school. The brass Chanukah menorah was shining on the kitchen table, its two Lions of Judah and the Star of David waiting for the first candle to mark the Feast. The house was fragrant with the freshly rendered chicken fat for Mamma's Chanukah latkes.

"Mamma, everybody's going skating tomorrow night. Can I go?" Mamma granted permission. "Go try on the skating suit."

"Who? Me, Mamma?" I couldn't believe my ears. "What skating suit?"

"It's your Chanukah present. I said for Chanukah...In the big factory box in the cupboard," Mamma beamed.

"I'll help you," Deenie offered as I bounced to tackle the box.

It lay there, almost alive, snuggled in rustling tissue, a mass of bright red fluffy mohair. A large red tam-o'-shanter with bands of red, green and yellow lay on top. There was a sash and a scarf to match. Mamma joined us, glowing with admiration.

"Next year, you, Dinyela. Sophela is older. Her turn first."

For once being older was paying off. Usually it was, "Sophela, you're older. Let her have it this time. She's still a baby."

There was no rancour in Deenie. "Take it out," she urged apprecia-tively, touching it gently. "Put it on. It's soft like a big pussycat."

"It has a funny smell," I ventured as Mamma lifted the massive sweater out of the box and began to pull it over my head. I sneezed.

"Heptchoo! Heptchoo!" I sneezed in Yiddish.

"*Tsun gezunt! Tsum lebn*," Mamma blessed. "To your good health! Long life!"

"Heptchoo! Heptchoo!" I sneezed again. Mamma responded.

"You see? You got a cold already!" From going without a scarf like I told you."

"No, Mamma! It's from the suit!" I shouted. "Heptchoo! I'm choking! It's from mothballs!" I struggled to get out of it.

"It's nothing, Sophela. It'll go away. You'll go outside, it'll go away. Till you'll come to the skating rink it won't smell already. Come, look in the big mirror how beautiful you look. A suchy year on me how nice it is!" Mamma was delighted with her purchase.

I held my breath and craned my neck to get as far from the smell as possible as I jetted for the mirror in Mamma's vanity-dresser.

"Look at me, Mamma!" I pleaded in despair, "I look like a horse! A big red horse!" I burst into tears.

Deenie put her arm gently around me. Mamma beamed.

"Twelve dollars and fifty cents I paid for it. Such a bargain. And why? Because it's from mothballs, from last year. In the big stores it costs *twenty-five dollars*! I should live so! That's what the wholesale man said. You should only skate in good health. Go. Go put on the knickers. You'll see how nice!"

"Mamma, I'm melting! Pull it off!" I held my breath, raising my arms to divest myself of the bargain.

Mamma was firm. "Go put on the knickers," she cajoled. "With both together you'll see better."

Papa was a fine tailor and the knickers were beautifully made. But I was a stocky girl, and while knickers may have been in style, they certainly didn't flatter me.

"See with the knickers?"

Deenie was beside me. "With Papa's knickers it's much better," she invoked his beloved image.

"Put on with the sash and tam and scarf," Mamma handed them to me. I obeyed. The broad sash about my middle, the vast tam on my head, I turned to the mirror and doubled up in horror.

"I'm an elephant, a big, red, striped elephant!" I shouted bitterly. "Now I can't move altogether! If I fall down I won't be able to get up! Everyone will laugh at me! I'm not going skating. I'm not!" I dissolved in tears.

Now Mamma was offended. "Shame on you!" she said slowly. "I would want people should laugh from you? Me? Your own mother? That's nice. My enemies shouldn't have such a suit! A beauty! And she's crying yet . . . I'm telling you, all the girls will be jealous on you. Some outfit! Like good butter. Try once. You'll see."

The moon hung like a silver Chanukah coin in the black sky. The powdered ice and mounds of snow shimmered beneath the coloured lights over the rink. The skaters were swaying to the rhythms of the "Skaters' Waltz" coming from the changing house. Red sparks flew from its chimney and the scent of burning pine-logs hung in the air promising comfort when the cold got too severe.

Me? I sat on the ice, spread-eagled, my new skates glistening in the dark. I couldn't get up. The girls pulled at my arms to lift me. The boys stood around and roared.

"Awright. Now – everybody together!" Bessie organized. "Pull, everybody, PULL!" I skidded around on my broad bottom but was unable to rise.

"You're pulling out my arms!" I wailed.

Bessie had another idea. "Hey, you guys!" she turned to the boys. "Come on. Help! You go in the back and push. Sarah and me'll pull."

But the boys doubled up with laughter. "POOSH!" They cried in chorus. "POOL!"

Bessie began to feel foolish. "Hey," she scolded, "Ya think we're your servants? Get up yourself!"

I wept with chagrin.

Finally, Hymie the Gorilla was moved to compassion.

"Come on, you guys. Let's give a hand. Sarah and Bessie pull and we'll take her under the arms."

I submitted and after several attempts, I balanced precariously on my skates. "Pull me near the house," I pleaded, "or else I'll fall again."

They took my hands and dragged me slowly to the rink's edge.

On the snow I managed. I entered the house and changed into my shoes and rubbers.

"That wholesale man cheated your mother," Bessie comforted. "This is a skading suit? It's more a tiboggany!"

"You're right, Bessie. But don't laugh," I tried to regain face. "My father – my father will buy me a tiboggany. You'll see!"

My skating career was at an end.

≈

∾ Diary entry [undated]

[This diary entry allows us to see the process of memory pieces that first appear in the diaries and that then proceed into a story.]

110

During the winter on Coloniale Avenue my little sister Deenie and I awoke in the morning in our three-quarter bed, feeling the weight of that extra overcoat Papa had spread on top of our blanket during the night as the cold air blew in through our open window. Papa was a great believer in fresh air.

Getting dressed in the winter was a long, clumsy business.

There was the white, buttoned, cotton bodice to which we would attach the garters of our long, ribbed, heavy stockings. Then came the long fleece-lined "combinations" which we called "*vesh*" a one-piece garment that covered arms to the wrists and legs to the ankles. It had a row of small buttons down the front and a tricky "trapdoor" in back for toilet convenience.

What a triumph it was to get into them! First the legs had to be pulled on, making sure they were straight so the top would be properly accessible. Next, the long sleeves had to be wriggled into and carefully buttoned so as not to skip a button and have to start all over again. Then came those heavy long stockings and the high black-laced boots. Oh, those high-laced boots with so many eyes, one was often tempted not to remove them at night!

Once dressed, the smell of hot cocoa and freshly buttered *kimmel* bread drew us to the kitchen where, in the grey light of the winter morning, we sat at the board-covered washtub which served as our kitchen table, tired from the ordeal of getting dressed. "Eat! Eat!" Mamma coaxed. "A good breakfast makes you strong to learn good!"

As the doorbell announced a friend who had come to call for us, we pulled on our red woolen overstockings, our snug-fitting rubbers, our warm overcoats, and the woolen tams and mittens Mamma had crocheted for us.

"Twice! Twice!" Mamma urged. "Put the scarf around twice. It's cold outside! And don't forget the little camphor you shouldn't get the flu!"

Tightly wrapped and bound so that we could hardly move, properly insulated by the hot cocoa and the good bread, we confronted the blasts of winter.

∽

MY FIRST PARTY

Towards the end of Grade Seven, our final year at Strathearn School, the girls of our class were invited by Miss Ethel Shayne of the newly inaugurated Neighbourhood House to form a club. The Neighbourhood House was a community project of the National Council of Jewish Women – a project established to keep the young off the streets and to integrate them happily into the community.

How special we felt! How grown up! Grade Seven, the graduating class! We had also begun to feel our sexual differences and there were signs of puppy love in the air.

That boy in the second seat, first row, was a nice boy. He was older and taller than the rest of us, a gentle, soft-spoken lad who loved to draw.

I was full of admiration.

"When he draws a tree it really looks like a tree," I told Mamma. And to him I said, "How can you make it so real?"

"And you?" he responded gallantly, smiling, but not looking up at me, "You write such good compositions. And poetry yet!"

When he showed me the drawing of an old sea captain he had copied from a tin of Old Salt Sardines, I was overawed.

"It's so real! His eyes like a real old man! And his beard…and his mouth with the pipe!"

Even our teacher was impressed. "Benjamin has a special gift," she said. I was very happy about Benjamin.

In our corner of the girls' basement, Miss Shayne's offer was very warmly discussed at recess and at lunchtime. Finally we decided to accept. The name Miss Shayne suggested for our club was the Merry Sorority. None of us knew what a sorority was, but Merry we liked, like in Merry Xmas. A girl named Frances, who had older sisters who knew about such things, said they liked the name. "It's like in College, they say," she reported to us. "With a nice name you could have parties and invite nice boys."

The Neighbourhood House on Laval Avenue was a pleasant place with airy rooms and banners of flowered draperies at the large windows. Miss Shayne welcomed us warmly and told us we would meet every Thursday at four o'clock. She also told us we would elect an "Executive" and keep "Minutes." She explained the terms briefly and added, "You will pay five cents at each meeting and the Treasurer will buy a book in which the Secretary will write your Minutes. The rest of the money will be for refreshments when you have a party."

Our elections were by acclamation and were based on logic. Because Frances had those knowledgeable sisters, she was elected President. Bessie was best in arithmetic, so was chosen Treasurer. I, Sophie, was elected Secretary because I was "so good at composition and poetry."

On the way home from the meeting, we all accompanied Bessie to Malo's where, armed with the first collection of five cent pieces, we bought a special exercise book for Minutes. I accepted the book with pride, well aware of my responsibility, and spent that whole evening after *Shule* fashioning the Minutes of our first meeting according to Miss Shayne.

As the time went on, I discovered the lyrics remained pretty much the same. Only the melody changed.

Week 1: The girls of the Merry Sorority Club had their first meeting at the Neighbourhood House. Miss Shayne said we should elect an Executive. Frances is President, Bessie is Treasurer, and Sophie is Secretary. We have to pay 5 cents a week for refreshments for parties. Frances said we should have a party right away. We will talk about it again next week. The meeting was adjourned.

Week 2: The girls of the Merry Sorority had their second meeting at the Neighbourhood House. Sophie read the Minutes of the first meeting. Frances said we should have a party. With boys. We have to have a house for the party. A few girls said they'll talk to their mothers. The meeting was adjourned.

Week 3: The girls of the Merry Sorority had their third meeting at the Neighbourhood House. Sophie read the Minutes of the second meeting. Frances asked which girl could give her house for the party. Nobody's mother said yes. We will speak about it again next week. The meeting was adjourned.

Week 4: The girls of the Merry Sorority had their meeting at the Neighbourhood House. Sophie read the Minutes. Frances said her mother said she could have the party in their house. Her mother will bake a big cake, and we could buy the ginger ale from the club money. Frances's big sisters said they would help with the program. The party will be in two weeks, Friday night at 7 o'clock. With boys! The meeting was adjourned.

Week 5: The girls of the Merry Sorority had their fifth meeting at the Neighbourhood House. Sophie read the Minutes. Everyone was glad the party would be next week. Some of the girls said we should have some boys from the class and some from the other Grade Seven. But Frances said Grade Seven boys are too babyish. She said we should invite some bigger boys – girls' brothers. But some of the girls don't want their brothers at the party and they don't know other boys to ask. So everybody said, "So let be with the boys from the class." We decided we wouldn't have a meeting next week because it's before the party. The meeting was adjourned.

I had kept Mamma *au courant* about the Merry Sorority party. "Ma, they'll come," I reported finally, "the boys from the class."

"That's nice," said Mamma. "So for your first party you need a new dress."

I was thrilled. Except when I heard that Benjamin could not come. He worked in the drugstore late Friday night. My heart sank. All the boys would be there, but not Benjamin! I dared not say a word.

Mamma kept her word and bought me a new dress for the party. It was peach coloured, of a silky stuff – a square dress with a short accordion-pleated skirt and a big rose hand-painted on the bodice.

Mamma was very proud of her purchase. "It's the new style – a flapper dress," she announced. "Good that we have a friend with a factory. Only two left, he told me. Put it on."

This was my first "bought" dress. Until then, my auntie had cut out dresses for me and Mamma had sewn them on her Singer treadle sewing machine in the dining room. Sometimes she even embroidered them with a butterfly.

"A grown-up dress," Mamma emphasized. "The rose is hand-painted. In gold yet."

Like Cinderella's sisters, I pushed and pulled. I finally squeezed myself into the dress, but it clung to my budding breasts and reached halfway up my pubescent thighs.

"Mamma, give it back," I pleaded. "It's not for me."

"It's the style," she said. "Flapper dresses are very short."

"But look how tight it is for me!"

"I can't give it back," Mamma acknowledged. "He told me they don't take back in a factory. He says he took one for his girl too – Essie, you know. Same age like you."

But age had little to do with it. Mamma's friend's daughter was a slight, sophisticated little girl who already used face powder from a "compact." She had shown it to me when we visited. I was a Borodensky whose daughters were tall, broad-hipped, buxom women and at twelve I was already showing signs of following the family design.

"I can't wear this dress!" I pleaded. "Look how short it is! My *pulkes* are sticking out! The boys will see everything."

But it was no use. I wore the flapper dress and stood in a corner all evening, hiding behind one girl or another, comforting myself with the knowledge that at least Benjamin was not here.

The party was not a total success. No matter how hard Frances's sisters tried, they couldn't get us to mingle. I need not have worried about my dress. I was properly hidden by the girls who clustered against one wall, while the boys clustered against the other. There was whispering from the girls' side and sniggering from the boys'.

Refreshments finally broke the ice. Frances's mother had prepared a lovely big cake with pink icing and we had bought the ginger ale. The table also boasted two dishes of raisins and almonds and a large bowl of fresh fruit.

At first all went well. Everybody was busy eating and drinking. Then the boys became a bit raucous. A fat boy named Issie grabbed a banana and, waving it at his friends, mumbled something. The boys began to laugh and to scramble for the rest of the bananas, boisterously comparing them for size amid guffaws of laughter. And we knew what that meant! One boy even dared explode the word "brazeer"!

We were mortified.

Frances's big sisters could not be seen. We could hear their stifled guffaws from the kitchen.

When we met on the next Thursday for our meeting of the Merry Sorority, nobody mentioned the party. My Minutes read:

Week 6: The girls of the Merry Sorority had their sixth meeting at the Neighbourhood House. Sophie read the Minutes of the fifth meeting. Because it is nearly end of school, we decided this was the last meeting.

The meeting was adjourned.

~

O CHANUKAH, O CHANUKAH!

CHANUKAH AT MY BUBBIE and Zaida's house when I was a child was a memorable celebration. Chanukah was celebrated with many relatives and friends, grown-ups and children around the huge festive dining room table. Zaida lit the candles in the large brass menorah as he sang the blessing over the lights, all of us joining together to sing the praises of the Maccabees, of Judah the Hammer, and to offer thanks to God for the miracle of the victory of our small, oppressed people over the mighty armies of the Greek rulers of the time.

When I was thirteen our Yedink Literary Club, named for the great Yiddish writer Yaakov Dineson, had its weekly Friday night meeting just before the Festival. We met in the Club Room of the Jewish Peretz Shule, and the topic of discussion was the Chanukah party.

Over the loud bombilation of our voices, our large-fisted president, Hershl, tried to bring the membership to order.

"SHA! SHA! QUIET!" he screamed, banging the table. "I SAID SHA! We can't discuss the Chanukah party with so much noise! AWRIGHT? So it's decided. We all want a Chanukah party! So it'll be next Friday night, seven o'clock, the night of the eighth candle. Right here in the Club Room!"

As our voices rose again, he again shouted, "SHA! I SAID SHA! We need a program!"

"Let's have Latkes! Potato Latkes!" Channah called out. "Yeah," we chorused. "What kind of Chanukah party would it be without traditional potato pancakes?"

"What else?" queried Hershl once the group had simmered down.

"We could have dramatic Etudes and Improvisations," offered Sonya, the star of the Drama Club.

"We need a menorah and nine candles," David spoke reverently.

"Don't worry. I'll ask my father," Faigie volunteered.

"What else?" asked Hershl.

"We could ask Yanya Eibel to sing with us," Leah suggested. She was speaking of Elie's father, our beloved *Shule* personality. "He sings so nice." We all voiced our agreement.

With no more suggestions coming forth, our teacher *Lerer* (male teacher) Zipper offered, "And let's have a Living Newspaper. With telegrams from the Maccabees and others, and some poems and other fun things you can all write."

It was a good idea, but the response to *Lerer* Zipper's suggestion was half-hearted since it implied work on our part. "I'll help you," our teacher urged.

Hershl banged on the table. "The motion is passed."

I had been listening attentively. Suddenly I exclaimed, "Let's all dress up like Greeks!"

A babel of dissent greeted my suggestion.

"Crazy!" yelled Dvoirah. "Where'll we get the costumes?"

I saw it all before me. "We'll ask our mothers for a sheet and some pins. Don't you remember the picture in our history book? The Greeks wore sheets!"

More noisy discussion. "Nah, who needs it?"

"My mother won't let!"

"Yeah, it'll be fun!"

"So ask your married sisters. She'll give you!"

Hershl banged on the table one more time. "A good idea! Motion carried!"

The matter of the "Latkes" raised another problem. Who would make them?

"It's too much work for a mother to make for so many kids!" offered Kraindl.

Sonya spoke up. "Shulamis, you and me can make them in your house if your mother will let."

Mamma said she would let.

On Monday, Hershl and I, armed with our collective five-cent club fees, went shopping for ten pounds of potatoes and a pound of sugar. Eggs, onions, baking powder and oil Mamma would contribute. On Friday, Sonya and I met after school to peel and grate the potatoes and prepare the potato pancakes for the party that would take place that evening.

We were in high spirits as we took turns, noting, as we grated, the periodic red stains that appeared in the basin as we accidentally scraped bits of our own skin into it, and mixed and stirred in the other ingredients. Finally, the house was filled with the memorable aroma of browning potato latkes, which we would serve with the granulated sugar.

The pancakes filled Mamma's largest basin. Sonya and I were delighted. We smiled at each other in appreciation.

"So now I'll go home and get my costume ready," she said. "I'll meet you in *Shule*. Gimme your costume too. I'll take it for you. You have to carry the latkes."

"Don't get them mixed up!" I cautioned. "My mother'll kill me if I bring back the wrong one!"

"Remember, it's for seven o'clock. Don't be late!"

A light snow had fallen in the late afternoon. As I pulled on my rubber boots, my heavy winter coat, my long woolen scarf and crocheted tam, Mamma called to me from the kitchen. "Careful with the *shissel* (bowl). It's slippery when there's just a little bit of snow. And don't forget to bring back the sheet."

The snow was white and lovely on the ground. The sidewalks were slippery, but I was very careful and managed to get to the *Shule* safely and happily with my load.

The earthen school ground was blanketed with untrodden

snow, but I knew that right beyond the entrance, there was a deep pothole. I treaded carefully, but stumbled right into it, flat on my face, upturning the *shissel*, and scattering the precious pancakes before me. I was devastated! Petrified! What sort of Chanukah party would it be without latkes? I looked around carefully to make sure no one had seen me, then I quickly picked up the latkes, brushed the snow off them and replaced them in the basin.

Sonya arrived shortly after me. "Good," she approved, "you brought the latkes."

"Yeah," I answered nonchalantly, "But we'll have to ask the janitor if we could warm them in his stove. They got cold already . . ."

The party was a success. The telegrams from Judah the Maccabee to his father Mattathias and from Hannah and her seven sons, penned by *Lerer* Zipper, warmed our hearts. Hershl lit the candles and sang the blessing. We all joined in to sing "O Chanukah, O Chanukah," and the other Yiddish Chanukah songs we knew and loved.

After a few minutes of trying to manipulate our "costumes," our white sheets, Hershl announced, "I'm taking mine off. It's no wonder they lost the war!" Happily, we all followed suit and dropped them in a pile.

The dramatic Etudes and Improvisations left us helpless with laughter. The newspaper, written mostly by *Lerer* Zipper, was a success. Yanya Eibel was his usual delightful self: singing the folk songs we loved; inviting us to join in, as usual; making sure to teach us a new one before he left.

And the latkes? They disappeared in a matter of minutes. "Good Latkes," everyone lisped as they munched, "Good and hot!"

Only Mamma wasn't impressed with my success. I brought home the wrong sheet.

119

Entering Adulthood

The transition from school to adult life was fraught with indecision – always a problem for the troubled Shulamis. During high school she visited New York City on several occasions and was introduced to Emma Goldman. Her world expanded and she saw many possibilities for herself. She wanted to go to New York to study jewelry making. Her introduction to Emma Goldman attracted her to the world of the struggle for social justice and what was happening in Russia; she was tempted by the exciting intellectual and theatre life of New York City; she wanted to become a teacher; she never ceased wanting to be a writer. She was drawn to feminist ideas and was unsure about whether or not she should marry, torn between her clearly romantic tendencies and a wish for independence and freedom.

After graduating from Montreal's Baron Byng High School in 1931 Shulamis attended Macdonald College and completed her teaching diploma. Although she received a teaching assignment, she postponed her entry into the teaching profession in order to study jewelry-making in New York City. She did not find the milieu she was seeking in New York; she was lonely, and she returned to Montreal. On her return, she resumed her ambivalent relationship with Ezra Yelin, which had begun when she was fourteen, and began her teaching career with a Grade Two class at Bancroft School. She was one of the first four Jewish women to receive a teaching position with the Protestant School Board of Greater Montreal (PSBGM).

Shulamis continued to be racked by indecision about her future. For major life choices and even the most mundane matters indecisiveness was a persistent problem and her inability to make a decision and move on resulted in constant tortured self-questioning and chronic extreme tardiness throughout her life.

TRANSITIONS

THE FAIRY TALE YEARS of grade school came to an end and all too quickly we were in the Real World of high school where our teachers repeatedly informed us that we weren't babies any more, and that the next four years would determine where we would find our place in the outside world.

Papa and Mamma agreed that I would attend Baron Byng High School, which was famous for a high level of achievement in the academic course it offered which included Latin, Music and Art. This course prepared students for university entrance, in comparison with Commercial High, which led to the business world.

Actually, Mamma had given in to Papa.

"How much learning does a girl need till she gets married?" she said. However, as the years progressed, it was Mamma who encouraged me to study.

Once again I was in a Protestant school where 99.9% of the population was Jewish. Yet, there was not a single Jewish teacher on staff. Even with a B.A. degree, few Jewish teachers were hired and those who were could only teach in the elementary school; they were placed in Grades 4-6, which meant they had a $50.00 per annum advantage over teachers with a one-year Intermediate Diploma from Macdonald College.

The years went by pleasantly. My literary bent, which had been inculcated at home and was strengthened in the Peretz Shule, flourished, even as I limped along in mathematics.

"Instead of algebra, her math book is filled with her poetry," Mamma reported to Papa after she met with the teacher.

But the world opened up before me. Girlfriends and boyfriends appeared, then changed as we tried out our different tastes in search of our own persona. I had a special problem: I needed friends who also shared my Jewish interests in the writers and scholars who came to visit, and in the Yiddish Theatre that was then at its height in Montreal – and there were few such in my class. I also dreamed of going to Columbia University in New York to study journalism.

The Wall Street Crash of '29 put an end to those dreams. The white blouse, navy tunic, and black stockings levelled our economic situation in the high school classroom, but the fees at any university spelled out the difference. Most girls would end up as office help or salespeople in small shops. The few whose parents could afford it would go to teachers' college in the hope of being placed with the Protestant School Board.

In August 1931, we had just returned to the city after the traditional summer in the country. Much of that time had proved a nightmare for me as I went to the post office each evening, waiting for the envelope that would bring the matriculation results. In August it finally arrived; I had even passed my math exams and had a sufficient aggregate mark to enter McGill University.

Yet at this time of year, which usually found me busy, I was at loose ends. I had been agonizing over my choices and what was possible, but was unable to decide which way to go.

There had been many conversations about my future but it became more of an issue after I finished the high school leaving exams.

"So what do you want to be?" Mamma asked again.

"You know what I want – but it can't be!" I exploded.

"My daughter has to be different..." She responded. "Maybe you should go to Business College, like the other girls, after all?"

I jolt. "Mamma, it's not for me. I don't want to work in an office!"

"You're not thinking of what the principal said you should be!" She looked at me in horror.

Mama was referring to the day our high school principal had visited our class just before the matriculation exams.

"Soon you will be leaving us to go your separate ways," he said. "What are your plans? Perhaps some of you do not even realize what you are suited for." He paused. "We who have observed you all these several years know your potential better than most people. Yet, which of you will come to ask our opinion or advice?"

I went.

First he congratulated me. "I hear you've been chosen valedictorian." I acknowledged the honour.

"I came to ask what you would advise me to do after I leave high school," I began. I was expecting the beginning of a dialogue about the Literary Life since I was known to be writing poetry and did so well in literature.

To my astonishment, he said, "You are so good at dramatics. Why don't you become an actress?"

He had touched a nerve.

How did he know my repressed childhood fantasy, the dream that awoke in me when I saw my first play, *Joseph and His Brethren*, at the graduation of the Jewish Peretz Shule? I flashed back to my tenth year when, fancying myself a great actress, I had slipped down those icy stairs on Coloniale Avenue. And then to my reputation as "star" at the *Shule* since the time I had, in one weekend, memorized all ninety-two stanzas of Frug's "The Sexton's Daughter" to compete for the honour of reciting it at the Chanukah concert – and had won! Did he know about that? There had been little opportunity at Baron Byng to show myself in that light.

It was different with literature, in which everyone knew I shone. I had replaced the first dream with that of being a writer. The memory of the book I had begun to write when I was ten flashed by. I recalled how I had dropped dear Beth Belmont of the Storms when I discovered I was putting her through the trials of *Little Women*. I still had that shiny blue exercise book with its first twenty-two pages covered in blue copybook writing.

I thanked him quickly and rushed from the room.

I can still hear Mamma when I told her.

"An actress?! My daughter should be an actress?! A fine thing! He's crazy! That's a life for a young Jewish girl?"

"I know, Ma, I knew you'd say that . . ."

"What else should I say?" She looked at me in consternation. "It's nice to go to the theatre sometimes. I like a good drama myself. But my own daughter should go on the stage?" Her voice trembled. "Such a life they have! *Na-v'nad*! Wanderers – always moving from one place to another. And family life? What kind of family life do they have? Whose wife is whose husband's? Feh! It's not for us." She paused again. "People like us don't become actors."

"You know I always wanted to be a writer," I offered my alternative choice knowing I was stepping on tenuous terrain. "I always wanted to go to Columbia University . . ."

"All those writers you met through the *Shule!*" she interrupted me. "The *Shule* put such ideas in your head. My daughter has to be different!" We were quiet for a minute.

"I know," she continued sadly. "I know you always wanted to go to Columbia and learn to be a writer, but who has so much money? Such a Depression! Better think of something else." Speaking to no one in particular, she returned to the principal's suggestion. "An actress he thinks she should be. With her poems and everything . . . If that's his best idea, better he should keep quiet." She left the room.

One Friday evening shortly after this incident, when I was visiting my classmate, Anne, she said, "I'm going to Macdonald College to become a teacher."

"A teacher?"

In those days Macdonald College, part of McGill University, housed three schools on its beautiful campus in Ste. Anne de Bellevue: one school for training elementary school teachers, one for agriculture, and another for household science. It had started out as an agricultural school for farmers, then had branched out in 1907 to include their children and their wives by incorporating the McGill Normal School and establishing the School of Household Science. Its insignia was a gold triangle on a green field. At that time tuition was free, but one had to pay thirty-two dollars a month (eight dollars a week), for board and lodging.

"Anne," I said wistfully, "You know there are no jobs, especially for Jewish girls. Don't you remember what happened last year when we went to apply for training as kindergarten teachers in answer to the School Board's letter? 'Girls of the Hebrew persuasion cannot be expected to teach the Christmas story with conviction,' the Supervisor said, and she sent us away, even though the Board was asking for girls to apply!"

"I know, I know," Anne replied sadly, "But I'm going anyway. My parents want me to go and I want to go. Maybe things'll change. Look, what else can I do?" She was suddenly angry.

"Maybe I'll go too," I ventured. "I used to make concerts with the kids in the country every summer."

"You'll be good at it," she replied without looking at me.

When I told Mamma that I wanted to go to Macdonald College

for teacher training, this time she was pleased. "That's nice. To be a teacher is nice. I'll ask Papa. You think they'll take you?"

"I'll try . . ."

Papa, too, was pleased. There was only the matter of the three hundred and twenty dollars for board and lodging.

Then the miracle happened. The factory above Papa's shop suffered a fire. "The sprinklers on my ceiling wet the stock. All the English wools," he mourned.

Mamma contained herself as best she could. "So what will you do?"

"I called the insurance. They know it's not my fault. I'll see what they'll say," Papa was his usual stoical self. I held my breath in quiet prayer.

On the following Monday, when Mamma answered the phone, I heard her say, "*Nu*, thank God, Philip. Now you'll be able to buy new materials."

When Papa came home, he said to me, "Send away the application to the College."

"But the money, Papa . . ."

"We'll use the insurance money. They'll give me three hundred and fifty dollars." He smiled. "Just enough for living there and thirty dollars left for the year spending money."

"But Papa, the money is for material! You have to buy material for your work!"

"Meanwhile I sent it all out to dry. Anyway, the wholesaler said my name is good. They'll send me what I need."

The tale ends happily. Papa's material dried out without damage. I was accepted into Macdonald College, and was off on the high seas toward a career to which I would devote most of my life.

~

∾ Diary entry November 22, 1933

Xxx is a thought to me, not a real being. Sometimes he spells freedom to me, release, – a chance to be an individual, a human being, even perhaps a super being. And at times, I see him as a shackle binding one to what all women have been bound, – just another screw in a horrible wheel that spins round and round at a horrible speed & evaporates the life, the desire to be alive, out of the world, out of Life!

I would like to go away with him to Russia, to a land where things are really happening, where people are alive, working for some ideal, something really vital.

God, – give me courage, – courage and wisdom, – to know what to do and to do it. Oh to see the light.

∾ Diary entry March 10, 1934

I have sought to assert myself. I have attempted to quell the storm, the unceasingly eating sensation that is in me, by keeping on the go. I am out every evening, –lecture, concert, walk, – something. I have even gone so far as to join Hadassah, after all, and yet, even though for a very short time I thought I was pitching at normal, I find I am nowhere near it.

I've also begun to see J again and that also has a bad effect on me. He gives me nothing and I feel absolutely no desire to be with him. I make him very unhappy when he is near me & even worse when he is away. I can't help the appearance of M's mental-picture before me, & every letter I get leaves me insane for a week. He has bewitched me with his mind, I fear.

∾ Diary entry March 17, 1934

Saturday, 1:30 am
Fire, fire is holding my brain in two lashing hands, torturing it. – fire that does not consume with one flame & devour all, leaving naught but ashes, – but a cruel demon, now warming slightly, now flaring up, now subsiding altogether only afterwards again suddenly to explode & with its sadistic fingers to torment into Life.

I am tired. "O to pass [cease] upon the midnight without pain!" ["Ode to a Nightingale," John Keats]

∾ Diary entry July 7, 1934

Kamp Kindervelt
... No one knows of my [crossed out] the depth of my pain save I who sit alone by the well & watch the drops fall one by one from the pail into the darkness.

There is something in the night that just wearies out my heart with its heaviness and beauty and its silence. If the scream that lies choking in my soul could but escape and free me from this spell, I would wish to pass away from all there is in life. This stifling beauty throbs with wordless stories.

∾ Diary entry Jan 12, 1935

Our grandmothers were taught that their will was governed by a good angel & a bad one; we believe that we are governed by our conscience, – if not by our sense of justice; the growing child will see it all as a radio mechanism of two stations competing with each other for the air.

ॐ Diary entry October 22, 1935

I look upon myself. I see upheaval. Seldom at actual peace with my-elf – seldom a smooth equally varying rhythm. Mostly up high it shoots or else very low. Confusion. Extremes with little clear vision. Lack of self-restraint. A desire to shock others with my words to see their reaction. An emotional turmoil.

ॐ Diary entry

Notes from a Transformational course with Ann Scofield June 26, 1992

In my search for individuation, distinctive wholeness, I have dis-overed a cast of characters who have claimed center stage, sometimes smugly in the spotlight, sometimes as adversaries, sometimes in multiple conflict . . . let me name my cast:

> Rejected infant, child
> Girl on Coloniale Ave, bride of King Sol
> . Obedient daughter
> Romantic teenager
> potential poet, writer
> teenage girl friend
> Teacher
> Countess
> Bewildered young woman – making wrong choices
> wife
> mother
> public figure (in community)
> non-widow
> intellectual
> bewildered female
> bewitched female
> community worker
> overloaded "dizel"
> Guilt ridden "sacrifice"
> Femme Fatale – lover

Compulsive flame
widow
critic
Master Teacher
Hostess
Role Model
Hungry Heart

~

LEAVING HOME

I DON'T RECALL THE LAST DAYS before my leaving for Macdonald
College in 1931. I don't recall where I bought those antiseptic-
looking white-and-blue striped uniforms with the separate white
starched collars we wore that year, or even when I sewed all those
nametapes on them and on my other linens. Surely Mamma must
have helped. I can't even recall clearly that last evening when I
must have been busy sorting and packing, with my beloved Deenie
proudly assisting me in the living room as I layered my possessions
into my newly purchased valise.

True, there had been high excitement, with Mamma on the
phone telling everyone the great news that her Sophela was "going
to collitch, the first in the family…"

Where was Mamma that last evening? Surely she was there, at
home, yet I can't place her presence in our midst.

The morning of my leaving is very vivid in my mind. Mamma,
who rarely got up for breakfast with us, appeared outside my bedroom, fully dressed.

"Come eat. It's ready," she announced.

"Just coffee," I said as I sat down at the table.

"Take toast," Mamma offered in a strained voice, "and a medium
egg like you like it."

"I'm not hungry, and we have to leave soon. Why isn't Papa here
yet? He said he'll take me to the train."

"If he said, he'll be," Mamma's eyes glued to the white enamel tabletop, my untouched breakfast growing cold before me.

"You want to tell me something, Mamma?"

"What should I tell you?" She didn't raise her eyes. "I'll ask you a question better." She paused again as though she were seeking the answer to the Riddle of Happiness for me.

In our bedroom, Deenie was preparing for school, lingering longer than was her wont.

"What is it, Mamma?"

(Which important question does a mother ask her daughter just before she leaves her home for the first time? I wondered.)

"You're glad you're going?"

"Sure, I'm glad."

"Tell me. Do you..." She paused again, then looked straight into my eyes. "Do you smoke?" she asked as if everything depended on my answer.

I was puzzled. This was her question?

"I don't," I answered truthfully.

"Your friends, do they smoke?"

"Yes, they do."

"You're sure you don't?"

"I don't." Then suddenly, "But if I'll want to, I will."

Mamma burst into tears.

What was this all about I wondered? I had tried smoking when my friends did, but didn't like it. I knew I had other things I wanted to do with my money. So why was she making such a fuss over it?

"Why are you crying, Mamma?"

"I'm crying . . ." But she couldn't finish her sentence for sobbing.

Suddenly I felt powerful. I was eighteen and I was leaving home. I must be independent; Mamma mustn't make me feel like a baby! "I'm leaving home and I'm going to be a teacher! I'm leaving home!" a two-part voice chorused within me. I jumped to wipe out the quavering one.

"Mamma! If I want to, I'll smoke!" I returned to my room in disproportionate anger.

"Such nonsense! I don't even like it!" I thought, but I refused to say anything more aloud.

When Papa arrived to take me to the station, Mamma was still crying. Deenie, who had not shown herself all morning, came into the room with her coat on, her books in her arm. She kissed my cheek and with a quick, "Bye, Soph!" she slammed the street door behind her.

Papa looked at Mamma, then picked up the valise.

"We'll go now," he said.

When I arrived at Macdonald College and opened my luggage, I found a note from Deenie. It read,

> *Dear Soph,*
>   *Please don't be angry with Mamma.*
> *She really loves you.*
> *Good luck.*
>
> *Love,*
> *Deenie*

I was stunned. Deenie had understood.

And I? I was too busy being "grown-up" to see . . .

And Mamma? Mamma crying? Mamma could no longer call me back – to tighten a bow or to pin a hanky onto my dress…

Social Consciousness

Shulamis had a highly developed social consciousness, which is obvious even in her early teenage years.

She attended an Emma Goldman lecture in 1934 and met with her in Montreal through friends. Emma Goldman became an important role model for Shulamis and remained so for the rest of her life.

Her trip to Russia in 1937 was a turning point in Shulamis's life. It opened up new ways of thinking and broadened her perspecives.

Throughout her life Shulamis found comfort and satisfaction with community involvement in groups of like-minded people. She was actively involved with Pioneer Women, a Labour Zionist organization with a distinctly feminist orientation. She wrote and delivered speeches at conventions across Canada, growing and developing as a writer and a public speaker.

From a very young age she was preoccupied by Jewish tradition, thought, and Jewish humour, and she frequently wrote and spoke about these matters throughout her adult life, particularly after her retirement from teaching when she had more discretionary time.

Shulamis also maintained strong ties to the Jewish Peretz School, and in her writings she refers to it as the *Shule*. It was there that she founded the kindergarten in 1941. Even when no longer teaching there, she maintained close ties with Jacob Zipper, the founding principal of the school and one of her former teachers, and she supported the school in every way she could. She was also involved with and supported the Jewish People's School, the *Folkshule*.

Shulamis was a founding member of Congregation Dorshei Emet Reconstructionist Synagogue of Montreal (1960). In the Reconstructionist movement she found a welcoming home for her longstanding practice of marrying Jewish culture with her intellectual and community interests and engagement. The egalitarian and social involvement aspects of the community that developed around the synagogue were very important to her. She participated in weekly services and numerous other programs and special events. In 1993, for her 80th birthday, she chose to have the Bat Mitzvah she never had as a young girl, as this had not been the custom at the time. She remained a vital and involved part of the community from its inception until her death.

Shulamis was a strong presence in the Jewish Public Library, where her papers are now in the Archives. She was also part of the Golden Age Group of the Saidye Bronfman Centre (now the Segal Centre).

She was very active with the Canadian Authors Association and participated in many of their programs over many years.

As early as the 1950s, Shulamis was among the first in her milieu to participate in interfaith panels on comparative literature and religion. She greatly valued and maintained significant relationships with leaders of other religious and cultural communities, and throughout her adult life she presented popular lecture series on multicultural literature, humour, and aphorisms.

∾ Diary entry May 3, 1934 [age twenty-one]

Spent the evening at the Bernsteins. Emma Goldman was there. Second time I've met her. She's just back from N.Y. They refused her the prolongation of her stay. She showed copies of the letters and telegrams signed by leading citizens throughout the States, asking for her to have her visit extended, but Roosevelt obstinately ignored her letter: When he was pressed for answer, his secretary replied that as long as Congress is in session they could not approve of it, lest they indicate the Democratic U.S.A. a haven for undesirables. So, someone motored into Montreal, 'specially to bring Emma Goldman here and to save her the expenses involved in the trip.

She will be 65 on June 27. Look at her – short, stout, but strangely energetic-looking woman. Doesn't look over 50, perhaps 55. That mouth hard [and] firm as steel, yet, how beautifully and easily it yields to laughter. A chin, made expressly for the purpose of butting against relentless walls. Eyes, deep set, behind a very thick pair of glasses, penetrating and rather tired, but still restless, contrasting strangely with the stout body. And such small feet! About size 3, it

Pioneer Women banquet, Montreal, 1945.
Shulamis, third from the front.
Jewish Public Library.

seemed to me. But they were heavy. But so small! I thought of her as in the picture at the age of 16.

We were discussing the subject of her giving some lectures here. There will be at least 2 at the Mt. Royal Hotel: The factors that brought about Hitlerism in Germany; the collapse of German Culture …[there] may be a third on "Living My Life". I'm to help organize them. Will have tea with her at her hotel on Monday.

I would like to stay with her awhile and hear her, see her as herself, speak to her of herself and her friends. I wish I could.

Emma Goldman has not penetrated me as far as Anarchism is concerned. It's not really for that E.G. that I would work, fight: it's for the E.G. who as a young girl had the zest to break away from a life that stifled and hindered her, & right thru her life has had the self-same zest to live her life as she has seen fit, never compromising.

"Back & breast as either should be"; always adding, adding, adding, adding to the fullness & her life & years.

Had tea again with Emma Goldman at the Ford Hotel where she is staying. We found her reading. She says, despite the heat, that one reads until 4 A.M. One has of late fallen behind in her reading. She must catch up! Sixty-five years old!

I ask about Russia: she said there is nothing there. "The only communism they have is the communism of Kings." Morally they are far worse. Much as in the time of the Czars. Formerly a man was sentenced to 2, 3, 5 or even 10 yrs. prison but when that was over, he was free to go out to his home & his people. Now he is put away in dungeons of excruciating barbarism, which ends only with his life. They are using dungeons & concentration camps now that haven't been used for a hundred years.

"And look at their treatment of Trotsky. Trotsky who created the [undecipherable]. Trotsky who has more knowledge & understanding of the International ideal than any other man living – they have not only exiled him & tortured him, they have even driven the other countries sheltering him to chase him from their […]. Trotsky was living peacefully in France. Then Russia whispered to France: you who are not at all favorable to Communism are harboring such an outcast?!" And Trotsky was told to "move on". "They will only be contented when they exile him into death," she said.

She spoke of education. "What good can it be, even at its best, if it gives the child only one point of view?" A newspaper published in Moscow undergoes six or seven series of censorships before it reaches Harkov [Kharkiv]! The child in Russia knows absolutely nothing of what is going on outside of himself & his little circle. Only one who has lived in it can realize it!"

Then at my question as to the probable ultimate reaction of the Russian people, she answered, "I have great faith in the Russian people, very great faith. . ."

Shulamis's trip to Russia in 1937 was a turning point in her life.
Jewish Public Library.

Shulamis the Teacher

Shulamis became a teacher in 1932, graduating from Macdonald College at age nineteen. She was one of the first four Jewish women to receive a teaching position at the Protestant School Board of Montreal (PSBGM*). She also attended Columbia University Teacher's College in New York City in 1939/40. She had a long teaching career; she eventually taught at all levels from pre-school to university. She was an inspiring teacher who brought into the classroom and the curriculum a love of the arts and her openness to cross-cultural folk tales, music, and art. She actively promoted an understanding and appreciation of multiculturalism to even the youngest of her students during their formative years.

Shulamis taught at many Montreal schools, including Bedford, Bancroft, Royal Vale, and Northmount High, as well as in various synagogue schools, the Jewish Peretz School and at the Hebrew University of Jerusalem. The Protestant School Board of Montreal conferred on her the title Master Teacher, an honour she received with great pride. Shulamis particularly loved teaching elementary school but really disliked teaching math, for which she had no talent. Her former students appear regularly in her diaries and many remained in contact as friends throughout her life.

*The PSBGM ceased operations in 1998 when the law changed in Quebec and the school boards were no longer organized along religious lines, but rather on linguistic divisions of English and French. Most of the assets of the PSBGM were transferred to the newly-created English Montreal School Board.

ᔓ Diary entry January 18, 1984

A letter from a boy in a Gr.9 Hist. class at Northmt. High, himself now a hist. teacher for 14 yrs! Remembered with love what I wore, my jewelry, topics I taught (his inspiration,) & that I changed his view from his father's attitude to understanding & sympathy for Jews. He married a J. girl.

ᔓ Diary entry May 1, 1992

2 younger women came up to me at different times, former students. H said. "I only had you for 1 year, but you changed my life. I became a teacher & wanted to be like you. I still tell my children about how you taught <u>Merchant of Venice</u>."

The other girl said, "I was in your Grade XI. You're one of the few teachers I remember from all my school years."

In the elevator at Dr. Z.'s, a woman addressed me, "You were my teacher in Bancroft School (Gr. 2), Miss Borodensky." She even remembered my name. Good.

ᔓ Diary entry May 5, 2002 [six weeks before Shulamis died]

Yesterday, at a Bar Mitzvah, an interesting experience. A grandmother, daughter & grandson came to present themselves to me: grandmother I'd taught at <u>Bancroft</u> Gr.2, my first school, Mr Perks Principal (1932-33), <u>Northmount HS</u> (1961-66), grandson <u>Young Israel</u> 1982-84.

Three generations! And I was there at <u>89</u>. The daughter was so thrilled to meet me. I had taught her in that great girls class <u>Gr. IX</u>, grandmother in Gr. 2, and grandson in Gr. 4 and all 3 came to meet me, <u>89.</u> It was fun!

Shulamis on the grounds of McGill University's
Macdonald College where she studied to become
a teacher, circa 1931.
Jewish Public Library.

GRIEVIN FOR BREAKFAST

How GREEN WE WERE! How parochial!

My roommate at Macdonald College was the daughter of a *melamed,* a teacher who prepared restless twelve-year-old boys for their Bar Mitzvah. Sema came from a strictly orthodox home where *kashrut,* the dietary laws, were strictly observed. Mine was a home where the only time I heard Papa and Mamma quarrel was when Papa insisted on using a meat knife to spread his butter, thus asserting his socialist, modern view that the dietary laws and all religion were the opium of the people. Mamma, who was also a socialist, nevertheless still sought to cling to the old traditions, and tried desperately not to mix any of the milk dishes with those reserved for meat.

In both our homes only kosher meat was used. When we went out to tea on Saturday afternoon at non-kosher Murray's Restaurant, what we had was tea or coffee and pie. Never for a moment had the question entered my mind of what we would eat at Macdonald College, a non-kosher institution. It did not cross my mind until my friend said, "I just won't eat meat there." I said nothing to Mamma.

On the first morning after our arrival at Macdonald College, my roommate and I were so excited that we were late for breakfast. Clad in our new starched blue-and-white, long-sleeved, striped cotton dresses, we were admiring ourselves in the mirror when we suddenly caught the sound of silence in the halls. I looked at my watch. "We've missed our breakfast," I exploded.

We looked at each other in dismay. "Let's go down anyway," she responded stoically. "Maybe we can still get something."

The dining room was a magnificent large hall with beautiful leaded stained-glass windows, and great solid varnished mahogany wood tables, which could seat at least fourteen people. At one end of the room, there was a beautiful marble fireplace, in front of which stood the table where the matron, the dietician, and other special guests took their meals. The rest of the room was lined with the tables loaded with the debris of the morning breakfast. As we stood at the door looking in, a waitress in a black dress with a small frilled apron and frilled headband came to meet us.

140

"You'd better hurry if you want to get anything to eat," she said, smiling, recognizing our predicament and our excitement.

She led us to one of the long tables halfway down the room. We sat down gratefully, smiling at each other expectantly.

She brought in two large dishes: one full of canned half peaches, the other a platter of toast.

"Canned peaches for breakfast?" said my friend in surprise. "Nice," I said. "Eat." At home we had them or pineapple slices for dessert on Sunday. As we began to eat our peaches, the server returned with two silver platters, a platter of freshly scrambled eggs and the other, a covered dish. I lifted the lid.

We looked at each other again in surprise.

"Smells good," I commented. "But…"

She finished my sentence. "*Grievin* for breakfast?" my roommate queried in surprise, referring to the Yiddish name for chicken-fat cracklings. "I never in my life heard of such a thing."

"Me too," I agreed. "But let's eat quickly. We don't want to be late for the first class…"

We both enjoyed our breakfast thoroughly. Who ever ate such a big breakfast at home? At home it was an orange, tea or coffee, and toast. Occasionally we also took time for cereal or an egg.

We ate our peaches, toast, eggs, *grievin*, and tea, and happy and full, we proceeded to the auditorium for our meeting with the teaching staff.

After the first class, my friend Anne, said, "You missed breakfast?"

"We were so excited, we came late," I replied. "By the way," I added, "The eggs were good and so was the *grievin*. It's the first time I ever heard of eating *grievin* for breakfast! But they tasted a bit different though…"

My friend, Anne, who also came from an orthodox home, gave me a scathing look. "Idiot," she exclaimed in exasperation, "What are you talking about? It's not *grievin*! It's bacon! You ate it?"

My mouth fell open. I had eaten bacon and had enjoyed it, thinking it was *grievin*! I didn't dare look at my roommate. From the corner of my eye I could see her rubbing her mouth as if to cleanse it of the unkosher delicacy.

"Let's go!" I finally whispered. "We'll be late for class!"
Neither of us would ever mention our first breakfast again.

~

I BECOME A TEACHER

MACDONALD COLLEGE! I revelled in its vast campus, its fine salmon-coloured brick buildings, its huge tapestry-like willows in which I sat to study or to write a poem. I loved my classes and was enthralled by the adult approach of my professors as they opened new worlds to me. The practice teaching sessions in Montreal brought both fear and delight as well as a vision of tomorrow. I participated in the extra-curricular activities offered by the Student Council and even had a boyfriend who escorted me to College dances.

Life was exciting, yet I was constantly worried; over and over again, the Dean warned that there were few jobs in Montreal awaiting the 167 students, and that meant even fewer jobs would be available to the 44 Jewish students.

Mamma was in great spirits that year. She even enjoyed better health. Like the other mothers with whom she travelled every Saturday afternoon, she arrived at the College on the western tip of the island of Montreal with her parcel of goodies, which my friends and I shared at our regular Saturday Night Ballyhoo Talent Show. This event featured extravagant dances on the cleared desktop by Mary, a girl with tiny feet whom I called Trilby, and songs by "Miss Manischewitz, the famous Matzah Soprano."

I looked forward to Mamma's visits but dreaded her questions. On the Saturday afternoon after my first practice teaching experience Mamma asked as usual, "*Nu*, so what's new?"

"I suppose it's OK." I wove between hope and reality.

"What did the Dean say?"

The Dean, that towering Scotsman of whom we all stood in awe, who, some students thought, delighted in humiliating them in the classroom...

"The Dean?" I hesitated.

On Thursday, during my practice session in Montreal, he had popped in to find my Grade Five class vigorously singing a folk song I had taught them. My conducting arm hung in the air for a moment while he strode to the back of the room, and stood there much like Hamlet's father, as I refocused myself on the children's rollicking refrain.

On Monday morning, before the assembled student body in the main lecture hall, while reviewing his visits in alphabetical order, he exploded in his rich Scottish brogue.

"Miss Borrrodensky! And what werrre you doing? The place sounded like a bloomin' operrra!"

The class roared. To hear of another's frailties before hearing of one's own lessened the tension, but how was I to take his comment? Was it criticism or was it a compliment?

"The Dean says there are very few jobs." I offered Mamma the acceptable non sequitur. "He says most of us who pass will have to take jobs in country schools." Behind this frequently repeated message lay my attempt to screen Papa and Mamma from disappointment.

One Saturday when we had settled in for our usual talk, Mamma said, "the ladies with whom I came both say their daughters are sure they will get jobs. They're better than you."

I shrugged my shoulders. I knew I was helping these girls with their projects.

Meanwhile, I was making a name for myself. I played the part of an eccentric maiden lady in the Drama Club's production of an English drawing-room comedy. I won the prizes for Dramatics and Public Speaking. I put together a musical for a girl who came to me for help with her project – only to see *her* win the Hygiene Prize for writing it! Beyond belief, I was even chosen to write and deliver the Class Will at the graduation dinner.

When the news of job assignments finally arrived, I was one of the four Jewish girls to be placed. I trembled as I made the twenty-cent Long Distance telephone call to Mamma – a most extraordinary indulgence.

"Mamma? Please don't faint. I'm phoning from College. I got a job!"

"What? What's wrong? Why are you telephoning?" Mamma was too excited by the Long Distance call to hear.

"I got a job, Mamma." I tried to speak calmly and distinctly.

"I'm fainting!" Mamma cried at the other end.

"Mamma, please...! I'm telling you I got a job! To teach in Montreal. For the Protestant School Board!"

"You got a job?" Mamma whispered in utter disbelief. "But you said ... you always said ..." she repeated, not daring to utter the negative thought. "When? Where?"

"This morning. In Bancroft School. Grade Two. A letter from the Superintendent of the Board! Nine hundred and fifty dollars a year!"

"Oy, *Tochter*, thank you! Thank God!" Mamma got her priorities mixed. "I'll phone Papa right away. He'll be so happy!"

And so began my teaching career.

~

MY FIRST YEAR AS A TEACHER

MY FIRST YEAR AS A TEACHER was a very exciting year for me. There were forty-eight Jewish children in my Grade Two class at Bancroft School. I relished the fresh, small faces that looked to me with awe and responded to my abundant energy and creative drive with appreciation and affection. There was a new sense of anticipation and order in my life and I looked forward to each day with pleasure.

Suddenly I was a child again, a child with a mission. Through play and games I would instill in my charges the love of learning I had acquired from my parents, from teachers I had admired. I would arouse in them the curiosity which drove me into endless serendipities, would lead them to discoveries that made each day an adventure.

I spent endless hours decorating my classroom, inventing devices to assist them in grasping the mysteries of words and numbers, opening new roads through literature and song, offering the wonder of making the conceptual obvious in something as intangible as 3+4 or 6x2.

Life took on meaning it had not had before. This was what I was meant to do and I did it with joy.

All my small gifts were brought into play as we dramatized stories and situations, wrote and recited poetry, created sets and decorations for the various holidays.

In time, I introduced *Children of Other Lands*, and even as we dressed the windows for Christmas and sang the beautiful hymns and carols, I introduced the story of Chanukah and some of the songs related to the festival.

The children felt at home in the Protestant school. The parents were delighted and the principal didn't object.

Papa and Mamma were proud of me and both Mamma and Deenie-Dorothy (who had grown into a tall, lovely high school student named Rusty) came on occasion to my classroom to share in my excitement and to admire the creativity of my "prodigies."

Shulamis's first kindergarten class (1941) at the Jewish Peretz School, with the students in Purim costumes. On the wall is a portrait of I.L. Peretz.
Jewish Public Library.

Shulamis with class at Royal Vale School. She brought a love of theatre and the arts into the classroom.
Jewish Public Library.

"Life took on meaning it had not had before. This was what I was meant to do and I did it with joy,."
Jewish Public Library.

SIMEON

SIMEON CAME INTO MY GRADE THREE class when the term had
already begun. He was a little boy with a runny nose and watery eyes.
He was small for his eight and a half years and he looked frightened.
He clung with both hands to his mother's worn cloth coat and I saw
his deeply bitten fingernails. He didn't look up when his mother
handed me his registration and report cards and said,

"He's been sick again, that's why he's late. He's had a mastoid-
ectomy, so he gets colds …

I smiled at the timid child, took the papers from the mother,
and invited him in.

"It's a new school for him so he's a little bit afraid," she said following us into the classroom, and covering her anxiety with a smile, she
added, "His grandmother died a few weeks ago. He's been having
nightmares about coffins and funerals…"

I winced but replied, "Please don't worry. He'll be fine here."

As I said this, the boy looked up at me as if to make sure he
could trust me.

I scanned his report card. His grades were poor. He would be
repeating last year's work. I felt sorry for the child but was repelled
by his physical appearance and condition. I sat him up front where
I could keep an eye on him.

He was distracted and frequently absent in those first weeks,
but gradually he began to adjust. He didn't make friends, but tried
hard to win my approval, and I acknowledged his efforts and called
upon him whenever he raised his hand with an answer. Often he
amazed me with his sensitivity.

Once, after a prolonged absence, he was very discouraged with his
marks and burst into tears. As the rest of the children filed out for
recess, he sobbed loudly, "It's not my fault! It's from the operation!"
He clutched at the mangled little ear with its perpetual wad of
absorbent cotton in it.

I ached for the child. "Please don't cry … " I pleaded, my hand
on his shoulder.

"It's from my ears always running!" he persisted desperately.

"So my brains run out from my head!"

"Impossible!" I said emphatically. "Nobody's brains run out through their ears! Or in any other way! You've been doing well, Simeon, only you've been away again. When you get stronger you'll do better. You'll see . . ."

"No!" he insisted in fury. "I'm just dumb! All the kids say I'm dumb and nobody wants to play with me!" And again he burst into tears.

"Simeon, I know you're not dumb!" I repeated, and, seeking definite confirmation, "I'll tell you what: Let's go to the office and ask the principal if brains can run out through the ears. He's the *Principal*," I emphasized, "and he *knows* about these things!"

He rubbed his nose and eyes with his shirtsleeve and looked up at me. I took his hand and led him towards the office. He stopped several times and eyed me cautiously. "Nobody likes to go to the office. It means you're bad!" he said.

"You know you're not bad, Simeon, and everyone knows Mr. Wilkinson is a fair man, and he knows about such things," I said. "He told me once that when he was a boy he wanted to be a doctor. But instead he became a principal." Simeon smiled and we entered the office.

The principal, Mr. Wilkinson, turned to greet us. Placing myself behind the boy with my hands on his shoulders, I looked directly into the man's eyes and winked. "Mr. Wilkinson, is it possible for brains to run out of a person's ears because he had an operation?" I shook my head sharply from left to right signalling the appropriate negative reply.

The principal caught the situation. "Of course not – it's just *impossible*," he stressed.

"You see? It's just as I said!" I turned to face the child. "Simeon says he's dumb because his brains run out from his ears since his ear operation." Again I cued the man.

"Isn't it true that when Simeon gets stronger again his work will get better?"

"Of course!" he corroborated. "No question about it! It just takes a little more time . . ."

The boy smiled weakly. He looked at me gratefully and we turned to go.

As the weeks passed, Simeon grew stronger and more at ease. He worked hard and liked to participate in discussion. He especially enjoyed the literature periods.

It was my custom to give each child an empty notebook at the beginning of each term into which we pasted the mimeographed sheets of prose and poetry I selected for their study. As the months wore on, the book grew thicker and thicker. The children enjoyed collating an anthology of their own, and memorizing and reciting the lines became a pleasure for most of them.

It was a joy to see how Simeon came to life during those periods, participating in the lively discussions. His still continuing nasal drip kept him from being a particularly gifted "reciter," but his love of words and his sensitivity reached the other children and gained their respect. He volunteered his opinions, often, to my delight, insightful and different from those of his classmates.

The year passed quickly. Despite the cold winter, Simeon appeared to be growing stronger.

"He's so happy in school this year," his mother beamed gratefully when she came to see me on Parents' Day.

"Yes, and he's doing so much better," I nodded. "I must tell you I really enjoy his comments."

"He was such a mess. You really put him together again," she said tearfully.

In June, at school closing, the children usually brought gifts for the teacher. Most of them brought bouquets of peonies. As I entered, the room was alive with the fragrance of these early summer blooms on my desk and the anticipation of promotion to the next grade was in the air. The children were dressed in their party best, their faces alight with excitement.

As I bent to lift all the flowers in my arms in ecstatic appreciation, Simeon came up and placed a parcel on the edge of the desk.

"For you," he said softly, and returned shyly to his seat.

"Thank you, Simeon."

I expressed my pleasure to the children for their flowers then turned to open Simeon's gift.

"Be careful," he admonished. "It could break . . ."

The parcel contained two packages, each one heavily wrapped in newspaper. The larger one held a green, glazed-pottery English teapot imprinted with a brick wall over which dangled the white-hosed legs of an English country squire; the smaller one contained the lid, the head and shoulders of the traditional Mother Goose image of Humpty Dumpty.

"A teapot!" I exclaimed, holding it up for the class to see. "Well now, I shall sit and sip my tea and smell my flowers!" I fantasized aloud. A ripple of laughter surged through the class.

"It's Humpty Dumpty!" explained Simeon aglow. "I picked it! My mother said *flowers*, but I wanted this teapot! I saw it once in the hardware store window!" he raced on. "It's Humpty Dumpty! It's Literature! And," he exulted, "I picked it and I packed it myself too!"

The children crowded around my desk to see better.

"It's really Humpty Dumpty," they said to each other in recognition. The little girl next to Simeon touched his arm. "That's a really nice present," she said shyly, looking at him affectionately.

What a triumph for Simeon! I looked at him in amazement.

"Thank you, Simeon. Thank you very much!" My eyes filled with tears.

"I'm glad you like it," he beamed. "I told my mother it's really special for you . . ."

My throat closed with emotion as his mother's words rang in my ears, "You really put him together again!"

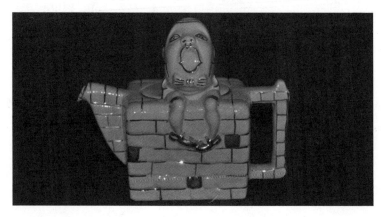

Shulamis the Artist

From a very young age, creativity and the arts permeated every aspect of Shulamis's life. She expressed her profound mental anguish in her diaries, and to some extent in her poetry, but her other artistic activities were more spontaneous expressions of beauty and joy, despite her personal suffering. She craved and was addicted to the public recognition of her work and her creations. No matter how many accolades she received, it was never enough to satisfy her deep-seated need for approval and belonging.

Shulamis became well known in Montreal as a writer of poetry and as a storyteller. She reported in her diary entry, April 1927, that the first poem she wrote, "The Fair Sad Maid," was published in the newspaper, *The Eagle*, in January 1921. She published her first poetry book, *Seeded in Sinai*, in 1975. In 1983, Véhicule Press published her book of short stories, *Shulamis; Stories from a Montreal Childhood*. It was re-issued by Shoreline in 1993. She received many accolades, honours, and awards for her writing. She continued writing poetry and stories to the last days of her life.

Shulamis saw creative possibilities in everything around her and everything she did. She worked extensively with arts and crafts. She did embroidery, crochet, knitting, and sewing; she made jewelry with silver and semi-precious stones; she created and exhibited stylized fishbone sculptures. She endlessly decorated and re-decorated her apartment. She took great care in the choice of her clothes and brought back from her international travels colourful costume pieces that she integrated into her extensive wardrobe.

She was a devoted patron of theatre in English, Yiddish, and French; she attended the Stratford Festival every year. She loved performing and listening to music – concerts and performances of all kinds – and played piano, guitar, mandolin, and recorder, and she also sang well. Shulamis loved to cook and to entertain family and friends, as well as her fellow writers and artists. She cherished these occasions throughout her life even when she was struggling to juggle family, teaching, and studying, often while experiencing great

Shulamis at Oka Beach, Quebec, 1954.
Photograph by Arthur Lermer. Jewish Public Library.

emotional anguish, and in later life as she also dealt with constant physical pain. Despite her occasional inappropriate outbursts, which grew more frequent as she aged, she was often invited out by friends and colleagues who admired her erudition, creativity, and joie de vivre. The stimulation and nourishment of these social situations was extremely important to her and she documented these social events with some detail in her diaries.

Shulamis was a popular speaker, lecturer, and commentator; she was a brilliant storyteller, always capable of telling a good tale and keeping the interest of her audience. She loved to perform and did it very well.

She traveled extensively: England, France, Israel, Mexico, Greece, Hungary, Romania, Italy, Norway, Sweden, Ecuador, Venezuela, throughout Canada and the United States (most notably California,

Diary, January 1927 – October 28, in which Shulamis mentions her first poem was published in *The Eagle* in January 1921.

Florida, and Alaska), and elsewhere. But she always returned to her hometown of Montreal.

Despite the recognition for her published work, she writes in her journals that she believed her private diaries were her greatest literary legacy.

It was in reading the diaries after Shulamis's death that the extent and nature of her deep emotional disturbance throughout her lifetime become clear. One can only marvel that this tormented person was able to function at all and was, moreover, able to live such a full creative life. It is interesting to note that so much of her storytelling and writing relates to her idealized childhood rather than to her own tortured reality. She transcended her inner hell to create stories that speak poignantly to the universal human condition.

❧ Diary entry October 13, 1983

Many people came up to thank me after the lecture – but there was that sense of aloneness after it. I seem to come really alive only before an audience.

❧ Diary entry January 22, 1988

Where is the keystone of the human heart?

For my Bubbie it was her <u>faith</u>, her belief that her God was in command & that her role was to march blindly to the drum He beat, for basically He was a God of Love, a God of Mercy.

For Papa it was his <u>hope</u> that a better world was in the making, a secular world in which man's care for man would ease the pain imposed by life, and that eventually <u>Justice </u>would rule & he fought for it to his dying day.

Where was it for me?

I had neither my grandmother's faith nor my father's hope. I had lived through other people's memories of pogroms & post-WWI social revolutions. I was a child in a secular home with spiritual (poetic) strivings I didn't understand. A home in which melodrama

Book signing at Montreal's Salon du livre. *Shulamis: Stories from a Montreal Childhood* had just been published. November 1983.
Photo by Judith Lermer Crawley.

was the recurring motif as Mama spat blood at least 3 x a wk, Papa acted as a part-time nurse while a hired maid looked after us; where friends who worked in factories came to Papa, a boss in his own small shop, to rage about conditions & tell about the union organizers who came to rally the workers to unite.

It was a quiet home, a home where parents never argued, where Mama rolled between lyric kindness & Yiddish curses that glazed my childhood blood. She gave me the underlying conviction that I was an outsider: 1. a memory of not belonging, 2. the growing knowledge that to survive I had to be quiet, obedient and, somehow to find a way of my own.

I became the introvert, the dreamer who dreamed of becoming (writer) famous. Perhaps a writer, like those whom I did not know but whose books received so much loving attention from Papa that they had the place of honour in our house: the place behind the leaded glass windows in our beautiful china cabinet of our oak dining room. There everyone could see & admire them.

I would find a place from which I could be noticed by all, yet

155

where I would be safe. Perhaps an actress like those on the Silver Screen at the Globe Theatre where we went each Sat. afternoon, my little sister Deenie & I, to watch the brave heroines suffer at the hands of cruel fate: while mothers died leaving children alone as orphans, handsome stepmothers who drove them out into the storm; heroines whom men used and abused in ways we did not always understand. Yes, an actress. And I lived my little life inwardly, bravely, moving to the slow rhythms of my body & soul, which so often made me late for school, which kept me from making friends on the street.It was in the Shule in the Jewish Peretz. School that the 2 dreams coalesced.

I sat in the dimly-lit classrooms under the gaze of Y. L. Peretz's last photograph, hung at the front of the school that was named for him. As I listened to my beloved teacher speak in her nasal, hypnotic voice of life in the Shtetl – that eastern European townlet which for a thousand years had harbored the fleeing Jews from all over Europe, had bred a cultural heritage in Yiddish, a newly-created & ever-growing, ever-enriching language & was eventually to prove its horrendous grave – I knew reverberations I could not understand. Could it be that I had lived other lives in those other times?

Kings in my lineage? Dreams in my past? Physicians & seers to other potentates? These were standards to seek to live up to. Yes, a book behind the beautiful doors of the bookcase, an actress playing the roles of her past lives, using Mamma's gift for melodrama, Papa's stoic endurance & yes, even tho' converted Bubbie's faith. (sic) / And then the Shule filled me with tales of poverty . . . Through the Shule at 12, I had begun to write poetry in English but found my voice strong & bright in Yiddish & encouraged by my teachers, was published in the annual school mag.

I entered and won an elocution contest to recite a 94-stanza [sic] ballad, "The Sexton's Daughter" at the forthcoming Chanukah Concert to be held at the grand Monument National Theatre. I had learned the 94 [sic] stanzas over a single weekend. [Because of the sacrifice of the heroine, the hero] lives far beyond the years of his contemps. to know not only the pain of her unlived life but the anguish of solitary survival.

This was my meat! Drama & melodrama. And I stormed the theatre with the words & the passion of my young heart. I was a "star", a leader, & I would recite at every Shule concert & at fraternal organizations which had learned of my talent (prowess).

At the English public school things were different. I was a quiet, fair scholar, sometimes very near the top at report time, sometimes very near the bottom of the class depending on how I had managed in Arith, a subject for which I had absolutely no understanding or memory. Numbers evoked no image in me. . . It never occurred to me or to the teachers to point out that they too had their place in fairy tales.

Indeed I was living in two worlds, a Siamese two-headed twin with a single body which carried it wherever it had to go. My active state was in the afternoon J School, my passive state in the public school where I was mainly an observer.

Life was difficult for me, the unusual gifted child. I hungered for friends but could not seem to make any. . . I stood at the edge of the crowd, looking, listening, but not belonging. In Gr. VII I finally came into my own.

❧ Diary entry April 1993

Creativity – the antidote to despair.

Writer's Block: Every writer knows it.

At her desk in her Queen Mary Road apartment, 1980s.
Photo by Judith Lermer Crawley, Jewish Public Library.

❧ Diary entry May 11, 1994

[Draft of speech on the occasion of her award by the Jewish Peretz and People's Schools CS, Place des Arts, Montreal, May 17, 1994]

This has been a bountiful year for me: I have been recipient of the Confed. Medal of Can.; have celebrated my own belated Bat Mitzvah, have seen the publication of the 4th printing of my book & now, to top it all, this cherry on the sundae so to speak. It is said No Man is a prophet in his own land. To be honored as I am this evening by my own community in the city of my birth, by the CS of the schools in which as a child, I found my soul, my identity & in which I was privileged to make a contribution not only in the J sector, makes this the high point of my life.

Family Life

Shulamis (Sophie) Borodensky and Ezra Yelin married on October 18, 1940 when Shulamis was 27 and Ezra was 37. Ezra (1903-1963) was one of eight children born in Bialystok, Poland, into a family with many generations of rabbis. He was educated at the Bialystok Gymnasium. The family came to Canada in the 1920s when Ezra's father, the prominent Rabbi Benjamin (Bunim) Yelin, was invited to head the yeshiva being planned by the United Talmud Torah in Montreal. Bunim's father, *Gaon* Rabbi Aryeh Leib Yelin, was a renowned scholarly rabbi. Ezra arrived several years after his family, learned English and earned a B.A. at McGill University. He was also a Talmudic scholar who taught at the Talmud Torah School despite his questioning of the existence of God. He eventually acknowledged his own atheism.

Shulamis and Ezra met in 1927 when their families became neighbours with adjacent balconies on Jeanne-Mance Street. The courtship of Shulamis and Ezra was a long one (thirteen years from when Shulamis was fourteen). Shulamis broke her engagement to three other men before finally settling with Ezra and there was some ambiguity in the relationship. Shulamis greatly admired and was in awe of Ezra's father and the esteem in which he was held in the Jewish community. However, Shulamis's father was a tailor and the Yelin family was not in favour of the match because of obvious class disparities. Shulamis yearned to be part of the family of this respected patriarch and was also clearly attracted by Ezra's intellect and his wit. But their personalities were not a good match and there were troubles ahead.

Shulamis was a native Montrealer who grew up with a strong interest in, and attraction to, Jewish culture and experience. She was formally trained as an elementary school teacher. An extrovert, she craved attention and loved the theatre, concerts, and the arts in general. Her diaries show evidence of great mental anguish throughout her life. We can see clearly in the diaries that from her earliest childhood and throughout her life Shulamis suffered from what we would now call borderline personality disorder.

159

(Top) The Yelin family. Back row left to right: Ezra, Sam, Hershel; front row: Shulamis holding Gilah, Nechama (mother), Goldie, Celia, Hershel's wife. (Bottom) Gilah, Shulamis and Ezra, circa 1956. The portrait is of Rabbi Benjamin (Bunim) Yelin, Ezra's father. *Jewish Public Library.*

Ezra was a quiet, gentle man; an introverted intellectual who was a brilliant scholar fluent in thirteen languages, and not particularly interested in social life. However, he was an active member of Labour Zionist and Bund organizations, and an avid competitive chess player and champion. While Ezra was entirely uninterested in social standing, worldly goods, and appearance, Shulamis took pride not only in her intellectual milieu, but also in the distinctive artistic style of her dress and home décor.

After they were married, Ezra – persuaded by Shulamis that money was necessary to support a family – embarked on a short-lived business venture with a partner: a wholesale dry goods store located on St. Laurent Boulevard. Ezra did not have a natural talent for business and when the store failed, swindled by his partner, he returned to teaching. In the early years of their marriage Shulamis suffered several miscarriages. She worked writing radio scripts from home, having given up teaching.

Predictably, the relationship of Shulamis and Ezra was troubled and difficult: Shulamis stormed and ranted; Ezra retreated into silence. Her already agitated inner life was increasingly tortured and, despite the social stigma of the times, she constantly sought psychiatric help but found no relief for the demons that plagued her.

Their only child, Gilah, was born in August 1944. Ezra's relationship with Gilah was loving but distant—he was undemonstrative in a typically Old World way. The relationship between Gilah and Shulamis was fraught with difficulty from very early days. Shulamis returned to teaching, at first part-time, when Gilah began school.

In the early 1950s two car accidents led to devastating physical consequences for Ezra, a tall, strong, and handsome man. There were also dire consequences for the family as he was unable to work. Ezra's legs first became paralyzed, then his arms, and finally his tongue. He became a complete invalid. He spent the last years of his life in the Mount Sinai sanatorium in Ste-Agathe. He remained mentally able until he died there from pneumonia, on March 3, 1963.

As the family's sole breadwinner, Shulamis returned to school in 1954 – studying part-time in the evening – to upgrade her qualifications in order to increase her salary as a teacher. She obtained her B.A. from Sir George Williams (now Concordia) University in 1957. She then earned her M.A. in English Literature from Université de Montréal in 1961, while teaching full-time during the day, studying at night, and caring for an adolescent daughter and an incapacitated husband. The intellectual challenge and stimulation of her academic programs proved to be her salvation.

Shulamis never remarried during the thirty-nine years that followed Ezra's death in 1963, although she had other significant relationships and opportunities to re-marry.

Ezra: Early Diary Entries

∾ Diary entry May 29, 1937

I knew that I should know him when I saw him. And I have found him and he is as I said – my love lies reflected in his eyes, his large hands spread warmth over my body, and his voice is soft and playful till it bursts my very heart. How I glow beneath his smile. My happiness escapes and flutters around me like a young, pale dove.

∾ Diary entry June 25, 1939

Ezra warns me to think well before it is too late but I lose more than I gain in the long run. "If man sins against God," he says, "the Lord may punish him in the 3rd or 4th generation. But if man sins against Nature, he suffers himself." Ezra is wise. He knows what he says. He speaks my language.

He warns me against myself. He insists I am looking for trouble in going away. "You will come back & then it will be too late to retrace your steps."

I wish I knew. It would be so good to be able to sit back & accept things & be satisfied with what is offered without feeling that there is still a straighter stick in the forest . . . without feeling that I am missing something all the time…

Ezra and Shulamis, Val David, Quebec, July, 1942.
Jewish Public Library.

After all, what is it I want? Yes, I do want to marry, to marry someone I love and who loves me, someone with whom I can march ahead towards a common goal. I want to work. To do creative work, useful, satisfying work, and have someone to share the pleasure of accomplishment with me. I want to have children, strong, healthy children with clear, fine brains, that I may learn through them, & in turn teach them not to be afraid but to dare to live & to learn to discriminate between struggling for fulfillment & wasting one's energy in useless unrest. What an order, – what greed!

Ezra's Death

[Shulamis was in Israel when Ezra died in the sanatorium in Ste-Agathe, Quebec.]

∾ Diary entry March 6, 1963 [three days after Ezra's death]

I think of Ezra with sadness and ache for the pitiful, unnecessary anguish of his life. Nothing came easy to him. This terrible illness with its degrading course for this strong man, who had never been sick a week during our marriage until then, - took it in his stride – always gentle, receiving his visitors politely and smiling, always grateful for the smallest kindness. He never complained and his wish for death was never flung over others. His stoic attitude acted as a buffer to those who came with embarrassment and pain to visit him. Everyone interested him, and he was grateful for every small attention. Death to him was truly a delivery, for life was a burden.

∾ Diary entry Friday, Sept 20, 1963

End of Rosh Hashanah. Home with G[ilah] & her friend E. Went to Shule both days, but today my heart or mind aren't in it. Couldn't even follow the service, alltho' X is superb. Somehow all my resentment of all the years of Yom Tov lost were in me today. Had a blow-up with Gilah yesterday when she accused me of abusing

Ezra in the Mount Sinai Sanitarium, Ste-Agathe, Quebec, circa 1960.
Even though the sanitarium was for TB patients, the family doctor
arranged a place for Ezra. The family could not care for him at home.
Jewish Public Library.

Ezra by asking him to drive me to R's party during B's wedding.
Brought back with a gush all of Ezra's ungiving self & all my hate for
him rose in my throat. I hated her for being like him! Dead tho he
is I wanted to kill him! Her inability to give to me of herself makes
me want to tear her apart as I would have done him. How I hated
Yom Tov, because he never contributed to it. Will I ever forget those
early Rosh Hashanahs when, the house shining, the table set with
lovely & good things, my husband would come home & refuse to
change his clothes! I hated him & still hate him for it! It colored so
many years of my life! It is in X I see just the opposite – his sense of
Yom Tov & beauty. No, I'm no longer in love with him, but I love
him – he is like an extension of myself & he is the spirit of Yom Tov.
Strange how deeply she can hurt me!

∽ Diary entries 1966

I must stop running. I haven't the strength for it. I've had the courage to suffer and not curse God and die or seek to die.

...

Shall I go to Esser's [Florida Health spa] and go on a long fast? Perhaps that'll help me cleanse myself and I'll feel better again? Shall I go to Vienna in search of Logotherapy? Or shall I undergo chemical psychotherapy here – shock treatment, insulin treatment, etc. & continue slowly to degenerate?

...

My own destruction lies within me – but Ezra summarized it at the beginning of our affair when he told me, 'You have too much conscience!'

...

I wish I were dead!

...

... yet something seems to have settled some in me: something has burnt out, but despite my recurring wretchedness I do have days of stability such as I haven't known before – or at least in a long, long time. I've been able to correct papers & teach & I do look better than before Xmas. But I'm not moving towards people enough. What kind of help shall I seek?

The Allan Memorial Institute

In April 1966, cumulative stresses catapulted Shulamis into a complete mental breakdown and she was admitted of her own volition to the Allan Memorial Institute of the Royal Victoria Hospital where she was treated for depression.

At this time, in her milieu, all forms of mental illness were considered shameful – something to be concealed at all costs – so her illness and treatment remained secret.

Three alternative treatments were available to her at the Allan in 1966: electric shock (ECT), insulin shock, and food therapy. She was horrified by the idea of shock treatment and it was never prescribed for her. She was medicated with various drugs such as Surmontil and sleeping pills. She was also assigned food therapy, which consisted of being fed "comfort foods" such as chocolate pudding many times daily, which was intended to fill the emotional gap experienced by the patient caused by a lack of having been loved. Shulamis soon recognized that this therapy was only causing dreaded, rapid weight gain but not alleviating her distress. She heard that a new experimental therapy, "24-hour group therapy," was being tested in the basement of the hospital and she had herself enrolled in the group. She spent five weeks at the Allan and three further months in day patient group therapy. These treatments allowed her to resume her daily life but did not quell the underlying rage and depression. Her illness continued to deepen and she grew less capable of controlling her often irrational and disturbing behaviour. The core issue of chemical and psychological imbalance, which led to the anger, guilt, and depression that had plagued her from childhood, was never resolved.

Shulamis sought many kinds of psychiatric and psychological help, as well as a progression of drug treatments, starting in the early 1940s and throughout the remainder of her life. Psychiatrists prescribed newly emerging drugs in an attempt to mitigate the emotional horrors so that she could carry on with her daily life. As Shulamis grew older, her illness increasingly manifested itself in bursts of anti-social behaviour that caused many difficulties in all manner of social relations. She sought relief and release from the shadow of her depression through the many forms of creative work in which she was passionately engaged.

In her diaries Shulamis reveals the extent of the emotional torture that began in childhood and stretched agonizingly over her entire life. Once aware of her dark secret, one cannot but admire her ability to function in the world at large, to contribute to her community, and to leave a strong creative legacy.

[Diary excerpts from the time of Shulamis's hospitalization at the Allan Memorial Institute, 1966.]

∾ Diary entry April 21, 1966

"Tales From the Looney-Bin"

Well, I've been through the valley of the shadow.
...

K [the psychiatrist] saw me at my worst. Thought I should come into hosp. When they called me I was afraid to go. I spent a week at home before Easter, then finally decided to go to Miami – soak up sun, swim, move about a bit. K said <u>NO</u> and I went anyway; wanted to escape both Seders. Was invited to X's for 1st & the 2nd was the M "Yahrzeit" at the syn, Seder –

So I went, & while it was lonesome and I was depressed, nevertheless since I came back I've been feeling better.
Yet here I am at the Allan. Doctor K said it's a chem. upheaval: an involitional depression due to Meno[pause]. "I can fix it." So, when they phoned yesterday I decided to go in & see what will be. "Stay a week – you'll feel much better!" they said.

∾ Diary entry May 13, 1966

[Written as she observes the effects of shock treatment on another patient.]

yet something seems to have settled down in me: something has burned out, but despite my recurring wretchedness, I do have days of stability such as I haven't known before — or at least in long long time. I've been able to correct papers & teach, & I do look better than before Xmas. But I'm not moving towards people enough. What kind of help shall I seek?

Tales from the Looney-Bin.
Apr. 21, 1966.
Well, I've been thru the valley of the shadow. But via Townsend, Edgell, Wittkower & Kral — all who did nothing for me, each sending me on to the next — Edgell, 2nd head at Mtl. Gen, saying the man for me is Wittkower, — international rep. in psychosomatic med, — psycho analy and Witt saw me but has no time, "an interesting case I would like to take on, — but no vac. now. I can't see you working with a young analyt, so, if you take my advice, I will arrange you to see Kral immediately, — & when I have a vac I will take you on."

Diary entry, April 21, 1966.
Jewish Public Library.

Somehow it's a terrible indignity to impose on a person, shock treatments. It's like the ultimate punishment, the rape of the ego! How guilty can one be?! Somehow, one almost feels one has a right to one's own devils. Why exorcise them?!

∾ Diary entry May 17, 1966

At breakfast we spoke of Guilt. The guiltiest time of my life? I believe it was when I walked into Gilah's room, infant that she was and only learning to walk, holding on to the bars of her crib & I came in and found she had had a bowel movement & was painting the white wall by her crib a gorgeous brown! And I was horrified: Text-book knowledge had nothing to do with me or my baby! She would never do such a "dirty" thing again! I spanked her properly, poor little baby! My guts still crawl within me & turn over as I remember how she curled up in a fetal position & didn't even cry! Isn't it wonderful that she overcame it after all and is able to paint? Ann said the kindest thing, "Well, you helped her get over that, didn't you?"

[Postscript: Gilah learned from a relative, only after her mother's death, that following this incident Gilah did not speak again for three years. From a happy, verbal child she became cautious, reserved, fearful, and detached, a child who carefully observed her environment.]

∾ Diary entry May 26, 1966

I'm afraid the stigma of this place will cling for a while, altho' I have no feeling about it myself. It's been a G-dsend to me. I've rested, am more relaxed, gained ten lbs & look well – all the things I came in for. All that remains is the decision- making again. How does one determine? It may be just the flip of a coin.

❧ Diary entry August 27, 1966

I've spent almost 3 months at the hospital in Group Therapy. It's been quite a time. I've fought against the pills – they seemed to do me no good – & am off them. I've unloaded a mass of anguish and repressed pain. I did not think such sounds could come out of a human being. The Yiddish ועיוון ["voyen"] has no real English equivalent: to roar, to rage, or rave is the closest & yet it is not just rage, which is anger or raging which is almost hallucination. It is a component of anger, hallucination & groveling, a composite which comes out of the guts of a hurt animal, hurt to the extent of the ultimate indignity imposable upon a crea-ture (created by God who created him in His image or by dint of his wondrous imagination.)

There were times when the sounds came with such physical anguish like a miscarriage or a sickness in the guts. There were times when the whole huge room with its 30 people – patients, staff & all – just disappeared, & I was alone in a cave of darkness, roaring & raging with my pain and humiliation. So much pain in one human being! So much anger & hurt & humiliation – it was unthinkable.

[The Yiddish "voyen" is usually translated as "howl."]

———

[In 2005 Gilah visited Edmonton and met with someone who had been a young psychiatric nurse during Shulamis's group therapy. B reported that Shulamis had "howled" throughout her treatment at the hospital and, with her constant shrieking, she had stolen attention from other patients.]

❧ Diary entry May 11, 1975

I have become a gargoyle
Rejoicing in the world's great pain.
I shout within and clap my hands –
Hurrah! You're wretched too!

Good for you!
Why should I have all the grief?
Why should I alone be mad at God?
My hate runneth over.
Yea as I walk thru the valley
Of the shadow of death
I am evil
Thy rod and thy staff they batter me
Though thou preparest a table before me
In the presence of my enemies
[...] pours from my every pore
And from many ways
My cup runs over, yet I am evil.
My cup of self-hate overflows.
Surely goodness and mercy will scoff at me
all the days of my life
as I live in & shall live
in Hell forever & ever.

ᥱ Diary entry October 14, 1982

And I remain alone, sometimes bitter, often angry, fighting with my shadow but never truly becoming one with it, except in the occasional poem.

ᥱ Diary entry August 28, 1984

I recall I began to write for "the other" when I was first alone. Over the years I cont'. to record dreams, which gave me insight into my feelings, incidents, daily chores, quotes from books I was enjoying, anger, pain at moments of happiness, often veiled, but actually the story is there – a prolonged issue, an autobiography.

Recently I've had lapses again. I have had over the years good & not so–good, recorded & not recorded. But I don't think I've used it to escape into illusion, madness. If anything, it has helped me avoid madness.

ᗧ Diary entry February 8, 1986 7.55 AM, Florida

[Shulamis spent many winters in Florida. There, too, she sought help from her illness.]

In a state of heavy anxiety these last 2 wks. Haven't written anything. Saw a doctor K, nice man, who told me I'm "on another plane from most people here" and suggested Desiryl [Desyrel], an elevant. I took 4 of them and dried out so badly, I quit.
Another panic day, his nurse drove me to a psychologist in Boca for a 1 PM visit. Again I was hysterical. He's a young man, warm, charming. After the hr. he said, "I'd like to see you again. I spend 10 hrs. a day listening to people – but you are different, so articulate," etc. His fee is $85. He said, "I'd like to offer you ½ price. Will $42.50 be all right?"

But I don't think I'll go back. It took from 21:30-6:30 to get back by bus. That was Wed.

ᗧ Diary entry April 1990

All that happens when I am with people is that a small bell rings sounding "tinkle, tinkle tinkle," barely covering up the deep low growl of loneliness in me!

ᗧ Diary entry July 7, 1992 [unsent letter to Gilah]

I try to go forward even as I go back. I want to understand & heal myself. I need to untie the knots that give me so much pain, to clear the congestions in my veins & arteries that hold back the lifeblood's pace.

I seem to have divested myself of the sense of love, that great hunger that I've always known for affection & caring seems to have been weighted down under tons of lead. It's almost more a memory than a live feeling.

True, I know <u>appreciation</u>, but love? I can respond with affection, but love? There's a heavy fabric of insulation about me that keeps whatever remains of warmth within me, safe from complete loss. But it also keeps me "safe" from allowing too much <u>warmth </u>in.

Gilah Yelin Hirsch

Hassia Gilah Yelin, born August 24, 1944, was the only child of Ezra and Shulamis Yelin.

Shulamis and Ezra were very different personalities and their relationship was conflicted even before their marriage. Shulamis was attracted by a brilliant and handsome young man from a rabbinic family of intellectuals. Ezra was interested in an artistic and gifted young woman who could hold her own intellectually. But he was introverted and shy and she was an extrovert who craved attention. He cared nothing for personal appearance, something that was of great importance to Shulamis. She was very physical and he was undemonstrative. It is clear in the diaries that Shulamis's frustration with the marriage and the clash of personalities between her and Ezra exacerbated her long history of inner turmoil and her emotional difficulties.

Ezra had said that he could not consider fatherhood while his father was alive; Shulamis became pregnant after the death of the Yelin family patriarch. Gilah's birth was met with mixed emotions. Ezra was happy but unable to express his feelings in a verbal or physical way. Shulamis was not content but the relationship suffered further from her own inner demons and a growing sense of confinement and restriction with her role as wife and mother.

Gilah's childhood was a difficult one. Her mother alternated tenderness with highly volatile verbal and physical abuse. The family dynamic was complicated even further when Ezra became an invalid when Gilah was eight years old. Both Gilah and the invalid Ezra were the objects of Shulamis's raging anger and frustration. Her inability to control her rage was especially pronounced at home. At school and in most social situations Shulamis was able to exercise restraint over the erratic behaviour, although this became less and less so as she

174

grew older. It was unthinkable at that time, and in that community, to publicly acknowledge any kind of emotional disorder – Shulamis never did so, despite many efforts to get professional help with her increasingly debilitating problems.

Gilah's Narrative

SHULAMIS GAVE ME MY FIRST DIARY when I was six years old. It was covered in pink leather and it had a lock and key. I began to keep consistent diary entries, filling one book after another. As my world was dominated by my mother's physical and emotional abuse, these incidents were recorded in the diaries. When I left home at seventeen, I left the diaries along with the rest of my childhood belongings in my mother's apartment. In the 1970s I asked Shulamis for my diaries, but was told they had been lost. When I asked again in the 1980s, I was told they had been found and thrown out accidentally. During a visit with me in California in the 1990s, Shulamis confronted me about the diaries.

"How could you write such things about me?" she screamed uncontrollably.

"You are saying that you have kept and read the diaries that belong to me, without asking or returning them to me when I asked? How could you violate my privacy, even as a child? And you know that, like you, the diaries were my only 'other'. I learned to write in my diaries by watching you write in yours."

My diaries were never returned to me and I can only presume they were destroyed.

―――

It is no surprise that Gilah left home at seventeen, never again to live in Montreal. Mother and daughter knew they would both be better off living apart. Though they continued to be close, there were frequent bursts of rage and abuse by Shulamis in person and by phone and mail. The diaries are filled with selective memory, pure invention, denial, unmitigated venom, abuse and contempt for the daughter she loved as well as almost everyone who was part of her life. Over a long period of time, Shulamis systematically destroyed photographs and professional press clippings of her daughter, including almost all her baby photos and wedding photos. In the last ten years of her life Shulamis would frequently make calls to Gilah, day or night, shouting, "You are beyond contempt. I wish you were dead," and then hang up. At the same time, there was also shared experience, love of the arts, respect for each other's creativity, and pride in each other's successes.

Diary entry November 22, 1938 [age twenty-five]

∾ I don't want to live a life through my children –I want to live my self, fully.

∾ Diary entry January 1984

"$64 Question"

When my daughter was five years old I took her with me on a short trip to N.Y. City. We shopped, ate out, went to the museum and art gallery, saw a great children's play.
    "Are you enjoying yourself?" I asked.
    "Yes, Mummy."
    "Are you glad you came along with me?"
    "Yes, Mummy." Pause
    "When you grow up we'll do lots of things together."
    "Yes, Mummy."
    We'll be <u>friends</u>!" I added for emphasis.
After a short pause, she turned to me and asked, "Friends, Mummy? What's wrong with being a mother?"

"Visit to My Daughter"
from *Seeded in Sinai*, Reconstructionist Press, 1975.

So I visit my little daughter in California,
and I find a woman
sure in selfness,
and knowing that her name is love.

Her home, reminiscent of the nursery
In which she first stood up
and painted murals with her infant feces,
is sunlit,
live with blossoming and greening,
walls aglow with works from her own hands
that mirror all her fruitfulness within.

And I can't believe my feelings or my eyes –
I the child and she my mother –
two worlds apart,
yet our shadows fall upon each other,
make strange interplay:
mother, daughter – single pod
split for further increase,
altered by condition of their separate soils.

Sunlight makes for strength
and luscious flowering.
Grow my poddling, grow and flourish:
I will breathe your fragrance
from afar.

∾ Diary entry April 13/83

It was right after another "flogging" & I was packing. I was numb.
She [Gilah] gave me the silk caftan dress someone had given her.
("It's not for me. I'll never wear it." "You have it for your book
launching," [she said].)

With Gilah at the launching of Shulamis' poetry book,
Seeded in Sinai, Montreal, 1975.
Photograph by Judith Lermer Crawley.

Numbly I put it on. It fit perfectly & looked beautiful.
"You look like an angel", she said.
"Get closer to the mirror. I'll take your picture."
Only in the mirror . . . with her image behind mine . . .

Or I "an angel", dead, & she able to step up into my place.
Only after his father had died did Ezra say, "Now we'll have a child."

∾ Undated Diary Entry - 1966

"What irreplaceable losses have I suffered? . . . And Gilah I never really had – not since Ezra first got ill. But maybe one day she will return; perhaps she's just too young yet."

∾ Diary entry June 3, 1982

Then on to the Toronto Museum of Fine Arts – where Judy Chicago was signing books re her *Dinner Party*.
"I'm Gilah Yelin Hirsch's mother," I introduced myself.
"Oh – a marvelous artist!" was her reply. Gratifying indeed.

∾ Diary entry June 11, 1985

Gilah at 4 – "afraid of the fishes"

Gilah's Narrative

THE INCIDENT, "AFRAID OF THE FISHES," remains vivid in my memory.
In the early years of my life, Shulamis's rage against my father and me was frequent and ferocious. She would uncontrollably smack both of us. When she ranted I took refuge under my bed with my two tiny pet turtles, my sole companions in my troubled childhood.

179

Ezra, Gilah and Shulamis, Grand Manan Island, New Brunswick.
Jewish Public Library.

I remember one weekend when my father and grandfather Philip went fishing in the Laurentian Mountain lakes. Both exceptionally quiet and gentle men, they relished the serenity and peace of the long, hot, silent days in the rowboat. They returned with large pike and trout for my mother to cook, and stored the live fish in the filled bathtub, where I, four years old, was fascinated to watch them swim. Some days later there were no fish in the bathtub and I was horrified to learn that the terrifying thumping in the pressure cooker was made by the fish being cooked alive. From then on I believed that my mother was a murderer of fishes and that, after dark, the souls of the dead fish haunted the dining room – the room that had to be crossed between the bathroom and the kitchen.

From then on, I was plagued with a recurring nightmare. I saw my father standing in a lake. He was fully dressed in a suit and tie, his shoes on the bottom of the lake, his handsome face, with glasses on, was crowning the surface. A toy sailboat floated past my father. A handwritten note that said, "You're dead," was attached to the sail. Ezra sank and was gone forever. I would awaken screaming from this nightmare. It was my father who came to console me. While this began and ended years before his debilitating car accident, at some level I knew that his spirit was being killed by my mother's constant rage.

Shulamis's physical abuse of me and my father continued even after he became an invalid and throughout my early teens. Shulamis's wrath never abated and as she grew older anyone who knew her closely became a target of her turbulent fury.

~ Diary entry December 14, 1988

I've always confused Gilah/Deenie, always call my child by my sister's name. Is it possibly because I didn't feel her being born? They kept me sleeping till the Dr, arrived, then he cut. I knew the knife but felt no pain & I was told I had a child.

Deenie held her when we brought her home. Deenie adored her.

Was that why I never understood or felt "motherhood"? Birth & appendectomy seemed synonymous – except birth was more painful. I remembered my "sister", just as Deenie was. My sister, except that she was really my "possession," my child.

Diary entry -Wed. a.m. cont'd March 20, 1991

~ Gilah called Mon. Am I angry with her? I said "Call me Mother! To you I am not Shulamis."

———

Deenie

Deenie was Shulamis's adored half-sister. Shulamis's birth father was Aaron Borodensky; a few years after his death, her mother Vichna married his younger brother, Philip. Deenie (Dena) was the only surviving child of Vichna and Philip.

Deenie was tall, elegant, athletic, quiet and reserved. She had a sweet and uncomplicated personality and was a beautiful shining light to all who knew her, especially to her sister. Shulamis often conflated

Deenie and Sophie. (Deena always called Shulamis Sophie or Soph).
Circa 1931.
Jewish Public Library.

and confused Deenie with her own daughter Gilah, particularly after Deenie's death; in her diaries she periodically expresses resentment that her adored Deenie is gone but the unsatisfactory Gilah lives.

Deenie Borodensky Aronovitch died of breast cancer five years after her first mastectomy. She left behind her husband Leon Aronovitch and their seven-year-old son, David, as well as a grieving mother, father, and sister. Shulamis never really recovered from her sister's untimely death. Each year she noted in her diary Deenie's birthday and the anniversary of her death, as well as frequently recording at other times her feelings of profound loss.

✿ Diary entry April 15, 1989

All my life, I have felt myself <u>the outsider</u>. I only remember my childhood closeness with Deenie.

✿ Diary entry December 1974

Today, 16 yrs since Deenie's death. 16 yrs!
Ezra envied her [death] … Gilah came home from H.S. [high school] shouting at the door: "Mummy: Deenie died at 4 o'clock. I hit the basket with my ball and the light went out."

It's been out a long, long time.

✿ Diary entry May 27, 1980

Today Deenie would have been 63. I met a friend of hers Sunday at Ruby Foo's Coffee Shop. She looked faded but energetic. Deenie wouldn't have looked faded, I'm sure. There was an aesthetic about her that would have kept her fresh & glowing. I still see her alive & bright & smiling. Such a great waste! I miss her with terrible fullness.

Shulamis, Gilah and Deenie. Sleigh ride on Mount Royal, circa 1948.
Jewish Public Library.

Gilah's Memory of Deenie's Death

1958: I WAS PLAYING BASKETBALL after school in the gym of Outremont High School. I threw the ball for one last basket as Miss McPherson, the gym teacher, announced that it was 4 o'clock: time to go. The ball hit a ceiling light that immediately went dark.

At the quick darkness, an image flashed through my mind, a scene from a historical novel that I had read. The doors of a crowded church in Quebec City, 1759, are suddenly blown open by a gust of wind and all the candles are simultaneously extinguished. The congregation erupts in grief as everyone knows that this signifies the death, at that instant, of the revered French general Louis-Joseph de Montcalm.

I caught the ball knowing that Deenie had died at 4 o'clock.

I walked home, opened the apartment door and told my mother that Deenie had died at 4 o'clock. I had previously not been told that she was so ill. Shulamis was shocked, called the hospital, and was told that Deenie died at 4 p.m.

My shock at knowing was even greater than the great loss I felt. Deenie was a second mother to me – the sane mother I did not have at home. We were both red-headed, with personalities that were quiet and introspective. She was consistently affectionate and loving, the calm in the storm for the first fourteen years of my young life. I adored her and was devastated by her death.

Mama and Papa Grow Older

When Shulamis's mother Vichna was cured in 1944 of the illness that had plagued her early adult life, she was transformed into an active and powerful force in her family and in the Montreal Jewish community. She loved to dance and sing and could be the life of the party as she had been in her youth. She was an excellent seamstress and designer; once she was able, she helped her husband Philip in his tailoring business. She was a gifted needlewoman, crafting fine knitted, crocheted, embroidered, and lace pieces. She became one of the renowned bakers in the family, with hallmark dishes such as Romanian strudel with Turkish Delight. She worked tirelessly to raise money for the Peretz Shule, which emphasized Jewish and Yiddish culture rather than religious practice. The school was very dear to her and had meant so much to her children. After Deenie's tragic death, she and Philip joined Deenie's widower, Leon Aronovitch, in the care of Deenie's seven-year-old son, David.

By the late 1960s Vichna began exhibiting symptoms of Alzheimer's. As her condition deteriorated, more care was required. She was placed in the Douglas Hospital (commonly referred to as "Verdun") and she died there on December 14, 1971 at the age of eighty-three.

Philip suffered much loss and tragedy throughout his life. The sudden death of his idolized elder brother Aaron led to his marriage with Aaron's widow, Vichna. He never fully recovered from the tragic death of their three-year-old son, Arele, and he was profoundly affected by the untimely death of their daughter Deenie. He suffered through the long illness and eventual death of his son-in-law Ezra, for whom he had much affection and respect. Vichna's advancing

Vichna and Philip on the occasion of their 50th
wedding anniversary, 1966.
Photo by Society Studio. Jewish Public Library.

Alzheimer's and move to the Douglas Hospital were very difficult for him, as was the car accident that led to a long, painful convalescence and chronic pain for Shulamis, his one remaining child.

Philip was a quiet, modest and reserved man who was unfailingly devoted to his family. He did, however, have a streak of the Old Country propensity for harbouring a grudge over many years; family feuds were common on his side of the family. In later years Shulamis was his only caregiver and by then she herself had endured much tragedy, loss, and she suffered chronic physical pain. As Philip's health diminished, the relationship between him and Shulamis became very strained.

In August 1982, as a consequence of serious health problems, Philip moved into the Maimonides Geriatric Centre, where he died on February 17, 1986.

Throughout her diaries, Shulamis noted the birthdays of her Papa, Mamma, and beloved sister Deenie – many years and even decades after their deaths. To these notations she often added memories and musings about her feelings for these family members who were central to her life.

∾ Diary entry December 12, 1985

Papa, you don't want help. You want <u>justice</u>. I told you <u>I'll get you help</u>. No, you want <u>justice</u>. Where on this earth will you get justice? Is it just that you should lie here like this? Was it just that Deenie should die at 41? Was it just that Ezra should have such a terrible life? That my life should be what it has been?

"You want justice? There <u>is NO</u> justice!" He nodded. He was feeling better.

∾ Diary entry April 2 1987

Today would have been Mamma's <u>99th birthday</u>. Strange how close I continue to feel to her, & in how many ways I feel I resemble her! Had she had <u>my</u> opportunities – what she could have achieved! And perhaps, had I had Gilah's, how much further I'd have gone.

❧ Diary entry December 15, 1986

When I lost Ezra it was relief mixed with horror. And then the loneliness set in.

When I lost Deenie it was relief mixed with true loss.

When I lost Mamma, it was relief mixed with the continuing horror of the memory of her long last shame of being in the Douglas [with Alzheimer's], and gratitude for her release.

When I lost Papa it was relief bloated with pain & anger, with love, & guilt of no longer being able to carry another load!

❧ Diary entry March 27, 1986

Thinking about Papa. Too bad he lingered those last weeks. Life was meaningless when he had that last pneumonia. It was meaningless before I left in Dec. He felt his time was running out & I felt paralyzed.

How strong he was! And powerful too. He had me tied to his will, to the end. I couldn't cross him. All I wanted was the father of my childhood! When does one grow up? I can't seem to work up enough enthusiasm to "live". I push myself into action. Even here.

I ask, as I asked Doctor P. once: What does it mean "to live"?

I saw them all die: Deenie young, in full beauty – certainly not looking like death was near; never being sorry for herself; dead after 5 yrs. of anguish – at 41. Ezra lingering 13 years, never complaining as he deteriorated, in loneliness, from 47 – 59; Mamma 3 yrs. Senile in that hell-hole.

Actually Papa died with dignity, but at least 2 years too late. Strongwilled, wanting to know … till the end.
 Only I am the sob-sister, perpetually.

LULLABY FOR MAMMA

"*Get her out of here!* Get her out of here at once or I'll have to throw her out!"

That's what I heard when I answered the phone that had been ringing vehemently as I approached my apartment door at noon.

"What's happening? Who is this?"

"This is Mrs. Robinson, sixth floor. Your mother must leave at once! She's hitting the other ladies! Shouting at them! The place has been in an uproar since she got here this morning! She must go!"

Coming down from the tenth floor apartment, I tried to collect myself. Mamma shouting? Hitting people? I couldn't imagine it. My clever Mamma, so composed, so gregarious! This should have been the best solution, to have Mamma in the same building where I could visit her often. What had happened?

Mrs. Robinson opened the door before I had time to ring.

"I'm sorry, Mrs. Yelin. She's completely disoriented and she's become violent. I wouldn't have taken her in had I known her condition," she added lowering her voice. "As you know, I'm a retired nurse and this is how I make my living. I accept only the well aged. These three ladies are very nice and sociable," she pointed to the three neatly dressed women standing in the doorway of the dining room, their faces blanched with horror. I recognized two of them. Mamma had often played bridge with them at the hotel of the Laurentian village where we had spent many summers.

I looked into the living room. There in a corner, in a small armchair, cowered my eighty-year-old Mamma: her still auburn hair in disarray, the look of a hunted animal in her sunken eyes. I froze.

She recoiled as I approached her. "Mamma, it's me, your daughter. Look at me, Mamma . . ." But as I tried to touch her face, to soothe her, she jolted and bit my hand.

I stifled my cry, pressed my hand to my side and tried again. "Mamma, darling, it's me, Shulamis. Don't you know me?" But Mamma only raised her hand to strike me, then drew herself back to get a better view.

"It's all right, Mamma, it's all right," I repeated softly, reaching out my hands to help her stand up.

"I – I want to go home," she stammered, as though she were talking to a stranger. "Where is Philip?" she looked about for her husband.

Home? Philip? Papa was in the Neurological Hospital for tests. The numbness in his fingers had grown progressively worse. These last months with Mamma had been just too much for him. I was teaching full-time. I was not aware of the degree to which Mamma had deteriorated. Nevertheless, the news that Mrs. Robinson would take her in had been a godsend to me.

"Mamma, don't be afraid. These ladies are your friends. You used to play bridge with them in the country." Mamma didn't remember. She looked at me blankly. Suddenly, she recognized my voice. She clutched at my coat, looking about her from the corner of her eyes, hardly daring to move.

"Take me home, *Tochter*," she pleaded in Yiddish. "I want to go home." I raised her and held her in my arms until I felt her body ease a bit, then helped her back into her chair.

"Soon, Mamma," I pleaded for time. "I'll stay here with you for a while."

"She hasn't eaten anything all day," Mrs. Robinson whispered to me. "Perhaps she'll let you feed her."

Rocking slightly to and fro, Mamma let me spoon the tapioca pudding into her mouth. She seemed unaware of what was going on. Slowly she swallowed the sweet creamy pap as I touched the spoon to her lips. After a few spoonfuls she seemed to relax.

I turned to Mrs. Robinson.

"What am I going to do?" I hardly dared voice the words. "My father won't be out of hospital for ten days and I'm at school all day. Don't you think she'll quiet down overnight? This is her first day. She feels strange here, she's confused."

"I can't. I'm sorry, Mrs. Yelin. Something has happened to her. It often happens like this. When they are moved from a familiar place they snap. She can't stay here. She's incontinent. She needs to be hospitalized. She may even try to run away. I can't assume the responsibility."

Papa, who had finally closed his custom tailoring business, was now at home full-time. He had recently spoken to me about the incontinence. He had kept it from me for some time, he said.

"But she makes everywhere. I try to keep an eye on her, to take her to the toilet, but she hides and . . ."

I could feel his anguish at having to reveal this to me.

I also knew of her "travels." On two occasions Papa had phoned me in panic. "I don't know where she is. She was sitting on the stoop out front. I was in the house. I came out to call her in for a cup of tea and she was gone. She's been gone over two hours!"

I rushed to their house. "Where can she be? What shall we do?"

But even as we stood there in anguished indecision, the door opened and in walked Mamma, fresh and smiling.

"Where were you? Why didn't you say you were going away?"

"I wanted to go home," she said, with that still girlish smile I adored.

This was 1968. The condition had not yet been diagnosed as Alzheimer's Disease and symptoms like the urge to return to the childhood home were not yet understood.

"I went on the bus far, far away and the conductor said, 'Where are you going, lady?' And I said, 'Home.' I gave him a ticket."

"But this is your home..." I ventured.

"Yes," she replied looking about her. "At the far station the conductor said, 'Come with me, lady.' He called a policeman and the policeman asked where I live and I told him 'Far, far away!'" Mamma was enjoying her adventure. "So the policeman gave me a ticket and he said, 'Go back on the bus till you get home.' So I went back on the bus and I came here."

Papa and I were thunderstruck. "Did you know the address?"

"I forgot," she said shyly, like a humiliated child. "But I recognized the corner and the grocery when we came here and the driver let me off."

On the other occasion a policeman had brought her home. She had remembered her name and he had looked up the address in the phone book.

Mrs. Robinson was right. Mamma needed custodial care. Papa had covered up for her as long as he could. What to do? What to do? To whom could I turn?

"Can you keep her overnight?" I pleaded with Mrs. Robinson.

"No, Mrs. Yelin. I'm sorry."

Quietly I coaxed Mamma out of her chair, and taking her overnight bag, walked with her to the elevator and into my apartment several floors above. In the familiar surroundings she relaxed somewhat, but her eyes looked hollow, with terrifying black circles around them. I placed her on the couch and covered her with a blanket. While she rested, I called our family doctor, a gentle and compassionate man.

"I'm so sorry," he said. "It's very sad. And it's hard to believe of your mother. You say she's eighty? She certainly doesn't look eighty! It's so unfortunate. We just don't have a cure for this condition, and," he added after a pause, "this happens to some of our brightest people . . . Senility . . ."

Mamma senile. Mamma senile?! This bright gregarious woman, still flirtatious, tall and straight as a die; always carefully coiffed, smartly dressed in those tailored skirts and suits Papa made for her, always wearing those clean white gloves she liked! Mamma, who always brought in the largest sums of money in the annual Peretz School campaign; Mamma, *Die Kluge Roite*, The Wise Redhead, whose advice was constantly sought – Mamma senile? For the first time I faced the word. Could the moon suddenly fall down and land in the gutter?

"What shall I do?" I asked the doctor. "Do you know of a good nursing home where I can have her looked after properly?"

"Frankly, there is none and it's impossible to get her into the Maimonides. They have a waiting list for years ahead."

He paused and sighed.

"There's only one place," he added after a while. "I know the name will distress you, but it's a good place. I go there regularly and I know they're kind to their patients."

He mentioned the mental hospital in our city – the Douglas Hospital.

A shudder went through me. "Mamma in an asylum?!"

"It's not in the lunatic asylum," he countered gently. "This is a special ward for women in your mother's condition. I'm telling you, it's the only place for her in this situation. And I know there's room for her now. I'll make the arrangements if you wish and I'll call you back."

My mouth tasted of ashes. How could I possibly bring Mamma there?

I had no one with whom to discuss the matter: Papa was in the hospital, my only child was far away in California, my husband dead. I had to act.

Two o'clock in the afternoon and Mamma was still asleep on the couch. I sat beside her as she slept fitfully. I had called my principal to say I had a family emergency and would not be back for the afternoon session.

At 3:30 the doctor called back.

"Get her into a taxi and bring her there right away."

"Doctor, I can't! I just can't put Mamma into the Douglas!"

"Shulamis, they're expecting her. I promise you she'll be well cared for. I go there every day."

Clinging to my faith in our doctor's judgment, I waited until Mamma awoke, then slowly dressed her. Where did I get the strength amidst all that numbness?

I called a cab.

"Come, Mamma, we'll go for a ride in a taxi," I told her, leading her gently but firmly to the elevator and down to the waiting car.

That haunted look never left her. In the cab, Mamma, who always loved driving, was terrified. She crouched in a corner as far from me as she could get.

"Where are you taking me?" she kept asking.

"You need help, Mamma darling. You need help to make you feel better." I felt like a traitor betraying his country. Would I ever be able to forgive myself?

A nurse met us at the hospital door. Together we led Mamma through the doors into the dark basement corridor. The nurse turned to me.

"You must leave now. You may visit in a week. She needs time to adjust." She motioned to an aide who came forward with a wheelchair. Without a word, she took Mamma's arm and seated her gently in the chair.

Mamma sat there, a lifeless image, empty of fear, a child in absolute submission. As I stood by, the aide pushed her away down the hall, singing a Jamaican lullaby.

A lullaby for Mamma! A lullaby for that bright vivacious lady, Vichna Dobkin Borodensky, the fiery redhead who, as she herself liked to tell, the small boys in the marketplace in Chernobyl used to chase, yelling, "Pozshar! Fire!"

The fire had been quenched. Only ashes remained.

~

VISITING MAMMA

I DIDN'T SEE MAMMA AGAIN until I visited her on the prescribed date. The image of her dazed figure, stiff and erect in the wheelchair in the dark basement of the Douglas Hospital, the gentle brown-skinned aide pushing her down the hall, singing an island lullaby, still burned in my head and my heart.

I had come home dazed, gone straight to bed and had slept hard through the night. Then, rigid as a nail, I had arrived in the morning to teach my high school classes.

The following Friday, Papa was released from the Jewish General Hospital. There was nothing they could do for him. The long years of testing the hot press iron had burned out the nerve endings of his fingers. That afternoon, after school, I picked him up and brought him home. When I visited, I told him that I had had Mamma committed. He didn't respond.

On the morning of our first visit, he called.

"What time is visiting? I baked her a nice big Cortland apple. She likes baked apples."

We were shown into her room. She looked composed and freshly washed, her combed, still auburn hair neatly piled on her head.

I stood by while this long-married pair looked at each other. Mamma recognized him and smiled.

"Philip," she said lovingly, touching his shoe with her shoe from the chair in which she was sitting, playing "footsie" with him like a young girl in love. We sat down and I watched as he carefully fed her small spoonfuls of the baked apple and waited for her to chew and swallow. Mamma's eyes were fixed on him as though I wasn't there. All the years of his devotion were reflected in them. It was just too much for me. I choked back my tears, determined that after this I would always go alone. I told Papa it was better for Mamma to have two separate visits. Papa went three times a week, bringing her a baked apple each time.

For me, visiting Mamma was the anguish of a snake pit. I could not know what she was experiencing when I was not there. Surely she was being looked after. Whenever I arrived, her room was immaculately clean. The bed was freshly made-up with clean linen, the linoleum shone, and there were no lingering body-function odours, though Papa had often spoken of her incontinence.

One Tuesday I happened to arrive before visiting hours. There, in the large common room, she sat together with a dozen other ancients. They were all tied into large highchairs, arranged in a circle, chattering away to each other with abandon, the mix of their own tongues and invented gibberish rattling on. I was also assailed by the screams and curses of other female patients who were segregated in side rooms, women whose pent up fury was finally allowed to come out. Incessant cries of "No, No, No," as if some indecency were being perpetrated on them.

Mamma was half-naked, tearing in a frenzy at her open-backed nightdress, trying to rip it off as some of the others had already done. Nausea and horror mixed with pity rose in me as I moved cautiously to avoid the puddles of urine all over the floor. I sought an attendant who could put Mamma into a wheelchair so that I could get her into her own room.

A shudder skirled through me. Could this really be Mamma? Mamma who was so meticulous about her person, her appearance? Mamma, who at eighty carried herself as straight as a pine tree? Mamma who dared to defy Papa, whom she adored, and continued to use lipstick and painted her nails with red nail polish? Mamma, who at seventy had been shocked by her aging face in the mirror?

I remembered standing beside her that afternoon.

"Look what's become of me!" she had mourned.

"Mamma darling, you look great! Don't forget you are now a lady of seventy . . ."

"So? Do I have to be so wrinkled? I feel so young inside!" And she tossed her anger to the ground as if to attack gravity.

I shot a glance at the woman sitting in a puddle of urine in the Senility Ward. This pitiful woman, Mamma? And suddenly I was on that famous game show, and the moderator was calling out, "And now, ladies and gentlemen, will the Real Mamma please stand up?"

If this can happen to Mamma, I thought, would it also one day happen to me? Dear Lord, don't let me live that long!

A nurse untied her, put a fresh garment on her, and I wheeled her into her room. A moment of recognition entered her eyes as we sat silently together holding hands.

When I visited again three days later, she was in her room. A lovely young woman, the wife of the attending clergyman, was washing her, dressing her in a fresh gown, brushing her hair. I remained at the door; the stench of urine from the soiled garments on the floor gagged me. I heard the lady say, "That was very pretty, dear. Sing it again." And Mamma, childlike and musical, repeated a little Russian folk song she had learned at her mother's knee.

"She remembers all her little songs," the lady said. She spoke in a gentle voice that had not lost its Scottish burr.

"She's really sweet, and she sings so sweetly," she added as she left.

I caught my breath. "My mother always had a lovely voice," I announced almost in self-defence as I recalled Saturday nights, the family and friends around my Bubbie's laden table. Everyone sang the beloved Yiddish and Russian folk songs, Mamma's clear contralto voice above the others. Such precious memories.

It was springtime and I was wearing a red hat. She looked at me for a moment and said, "I would like a hat just like yours." She reached out her hand. I took the hat off my head and handed it to her. She patted it carefully. "Mamma darling, when you are better, I will buy you one just like this one." She smiled happily and handed it back to me. "Thank you," she said.

By the third year of her hospitalization, Mamma had become quite vague. She did not remember me at all.

One morning in November, about a month before Chanukah, Papa called.

"Mamma is in a coma."

"Let it be over soon," I prayed out loud.

"Will you come?"

"No," I replied. "There's nothing to do but wait." But I couldn't wait. I went that afternoon.

There she lay in her clean white bed, her soft auburn hair with its wisps of white at the temples swept away from her soft pale face, sleeping peacefully as she had perhaps not slept in years. But there were all sorts of tubes and wires attached to her. I sat beside her, sick with congealed love. No words formed themselves in my head. I sat for a timeless while, then unknowing, got up and left.

Every morning Papa phoned, "She's still sleeping. Will you go?"

At the end of the week I went alone.

She was just as I had seen her before. I spoke to her, hoping she could hear and understand words I had not been able to speak in all that time.

"Mamma darling," I sobbed, "I love you. It's so unfair that you should linger like this . . . You've had more than your share of pain and humiliation . . ."

The doctor who was passing must have heard me. He came in.

"Why do you let her continue like this?" I stormed. "Why do you hold back her delivery from this hell with all those useless tubes? Why don't you pull them out and release her?!"

"*You* pull them out," he said with an enigmatic smile, and walked out.

Mamma died in December on the second day of Chanukah. Papa phoned to tell me. All I could say was, "Thank God it's over!" There were no tears. I had mourned too long.

Chanukah, the eight-day winter Festival of Lights, the holiday celebrating an ancient victory of our people over a mighty tyrant, had always illuminated our lives. Now it was marked with the commemoration of the dead. My young sister Deenie had died ten years earlier two days before the festival, now Mamma two days into the festival.

As I sat listening to Papa and grappling with my feelings, earlier Chanukahs flooded into awareness, childhood celebrations in my

Bubbie and Zaida's home on Cadieux Street, with all the aunties and the uncles, cousins and friends waiting for Zaida to light the old brass *Chanukia*) with its coloured candles, waiting to hear him chant the blessings and to join him in the singing of *Moaz Tsur*, Rock of Ages.

I remembered Mamma, her face alight with the festival, alive with that sense of gratitude and belonging.

As that memory reel came to an end, two Chanukah songs we had learned in the Yiddish afternoon school I had attended resounded in my ears. One began with the lines:

Who can retell
the tales that befell us,
Who can count them?

And the words of the song addressed to the twinkling candles:

Oh, you little candles bright,
what brave tales you tell tonight,
Stories without end...

Mamma's story did not end with her dying. Mamma's memory is alive today in her daughter, in her granddaughter, in the good name she left behind. She has joined the ranks of those myriad women, from ancient days to our own, of whom it has been said,

"A woman of valour
who can tell her worth?
Her price is above rubies."

~

NO MODERN MOTHERS

I WAS TAKING MY FIRST TRIP to Europe. A multitude of friends and relatives were seeing me off at Montreal's Windsor Station. I was to take the boat for Marseilles from New York. Everyone embraced me and wished me well. Mamma stood by and wept. Beside her stood Papa, embarrassed by such a display of emotion. I turned to Mamma.

"Gosh, Mamma," I tried to be amusing, "I'm not *leaving for America*! I'm not running away from *Fonya's* Russia! This is a pleasure trip! I'll be back in two months!"

But Mamma continued to weep. "I know… I know…" she sobbed. "Don't laugh. I can still hear my mother calling. Vichnala! Vickhnala! I'll never see you again!" Her shoulders heaved with weeping.

"Mamma," I continued gently, "She was an *old-fashioned* mother. You're modern. You're *now*!"

"Maybe there are no modern mothers," she answered, blotting her eyes with her handkerchief.

"Oh, Mamma!" I was exasperated.

"Wait, Sophela," Mamma suddenly smiled through her tears, "One day you'll be a mother too . . ."

And now I am a mother, the mother of a daughter who lives far away. We meet for a few days once a year. I seem to have made peace with this state of affairs. That longing which over the years I have masked with busyness, has finally come out in poems I have written.

> …and I, from lengthy fasting
> feel no hunger,
> or just a random memory
> of what hunger used to be…
>
> and again, with gratitude and acceptance, I think,
> …grow, my poddling,
> grow and flourish,
> I will breathe
> your fragrance
> from afar…

Why then does it happen every time we come together? There is great anticipation before she comes. I shop, prepare, cook, and plan. We meet, we embrace, and we are thrilled to see each other. We talk long and intimately for a day or two and into the night – two independent, searching women and that iceberg in me begins to feel as if it would really melt.

Suddenly I am uneasy. Time is slipping by so quickly! Soon she'll be gone again! That dissolving lump within me is congealing again! I keep swallowing to mask my tears.

"Mamma, what's wrong?"

"Nothing . . ."

"You seem to be crying."

"Not really…"

"Mamma, I know you. It's always like this before I have to leave!" She puts her arm around me. I weep.

"Mamma, I'm not leaving forever! We'll meet again next summer…"

"I'm sorry. I can't help it. I know it's silly, but I just can't help it… You're no sooner here than you are already leaving. So little time – and I have to share you with your friends!" The truth explodes from my mouth.

"But they want to see me too . . ."

I know I'm being illogical, cantankerous, and quarrelsome. I know I'm unreasonable and infantile. I know, yet I continue to sob.

"Mamma, I don't understand you," she says softly. You used to laugh at *your* mother for being *old-fashioned, emotional*. And now?

I hold my grown daughter close and fondle her auburn hair. My eyes overflow from that partially thawed iceberg within me. And now it is my own turn to smile through tears as I repeat, "Maybe there are no modern mothers . . ."

Struggles and Old Age

Shulamis's Accident

On July 1, 1969 Shulamis Yelin was seriously injured in a near-fatal car accident near Hawkesbury, Ontario. When she awoke from a coma after two weeks, she recounted to her daughter at her bedside that she had been at a Heavenly Tribunal where she was given the choice of death or a creative rebirth into life accompanied by physical pain. She chose life. She was hospitalized in Montreal until June 1970, during which time she had many reconstructive surgeries and learned to walk again. But for the remainder of her life she suffered severe chronic pain in her back, legs, feet, and abdomen.

During her long hospitalization she underwent a "creative rebirth," which prompted her to return to writing poetry and stories. The accident ended her teaching career but allowed her, in retirement, to devote more time and energy to her writing, both prose and poetry, and other creative work that became increasingly important to her and which she continued until her death in 2002.

Growing Old

Shulamis was endlessly concerned about growing older, even in her youth. The physical appearances and consequences of aging were distressing to her, but at the same time she did not wish to return to the difficulties of her early life.

She often wrote in her diaries about growing old and about death. As she aged, she became more lonely and isolated as friends and companions disappeared from her life, from illness, incapacity, death, and alienation. The emotional torments she suffered throughout her life continued and became more outwardly visible in her old age as she became increasingly unable to control the surges of frustration, rage, and anxiety that had always been part of her emotional life. She became more agitated and unpredictable, very often acting out of paranoia and frustration, and very sadly often abusing and alienating people in her social circles.

❧ Diary entry Sunday, July 13, 1969 13th day Royal Victoria Hospital, leaning on my cast

Despite the fact I had had the car at Renault on Mon. 8 a.m. & left it until 5:15 for its 300 mi. check up, I discovered just out of Hawkesbury it had lost its wheel control. It was only minutes after I had stopped for a coffee at the ½ Way House, taken a walk & a new lease on adventure & began to again drive. Suddenly the wheel became unsure. It had always been wonderful before the check up. Before I could turn off the road a large car had accordioned me . . . Blood filled the car. All seats and under the wheel were smashed. I didn't even hurt. I just thought – let it be over.

Soon as I was hit I heard a man shout, "I saw it happen." Apparently I had a blow-out . . . .

❧ Diary entry Sat, July 19th, 1969 7 PM

Lord, you've tried in many ways to teach me gratitude again. Maybe now I'll lose some of my bitterness in my struggle for life. I didn't try to take my life but my whole attitude towards it was like a flyleaf. I've been emotionally weary too long. So much anger at repeated & intensified responsibility. So much resentment at the classroom sit. & the lack of courage to leave it for a "secure future".

Well, ironically enough I got my wish. I shan't be teaching next year, & I need have no guilt feelings about it. But the physical suffering will be long & high. But for a time it will stop me running and maybe in time some true wisdom will enter my soul. Words I have, and some knowledge, but the ability to blend them with some mercy for myself can only come if I stop this flight & work at penetration in depth.

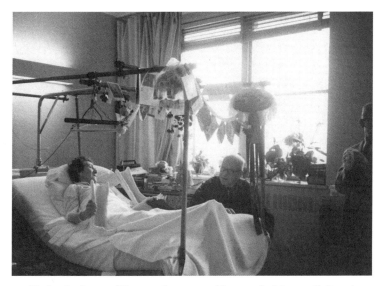

Shulamis shows off her newly-removed leg cast in Montreal's Royal
Victoria Hospital with Philip, September 1969.
Photo by Kay Wolofsky. Jewish Public Library.

∽ Diary entry July 23, 1969

I said to Dr. B in a fury the other day, "But Dr. I've been here 38
days."

"My dear Mrs. Yelin," he said, your kind of illness is not judged in
weeks but in months!" I find it hard to really absorb that a summer
passes me by and I be flat and helpless, nailed to my bed with
enormous cast. To the anguish of all the harm – and I have more
drugs & foreign blood in me than I have anything of my own. Add
the indignities of having your bottom washed of feces, the many
tubes that connect you artificially to life thru your nose, your vagina,
your veins – you feel like Steinberg's butcher shop dept. And it's
only a split moment of sanity that keeps you from vomiting out all
the goodness that is allegedly being given to you.

In Florida, 2000, where Shulamis went during
the coldest parts of the winter.

❧ Diary entry Thursday, Jan 1, 1970 New Year's Day

Well, today is New Year's Day & I celebrate it at the Jewish Conva-
lescent Hosp. in Chomedy, Que. Today I am 6 months old. Happy
Birthday. May the next 6 see me walking without artificial props –
well enough to begin to participate in life again. (I've actually begun
already: have been asked by Miss Sadler to review "Grandmother
Came from Dworitz" for the Congress Bulletin), and let my children
be better entrenched in their chosen field and all is content to live
together. And may life not be too difficult for my father & friends.

What a decade it's been: moon landing, isolation of the gene, heart
transplant, youth revolts, Quebec in upheaval, drugs, Israel's struggle
and the Six-Day War – my own liberation from Ezra's illness and
the searching years, Gilah's marriage and growth, and my parents'
aging...and all climaxed by the accident July 1st – my strange return from the cemetery gates, my retirement from the school board
(with honor) – two years earlier than I dared hope – and for all my

destruction a resurrection with good friends and tomorrow looking less frightening than before. May it be ever so.

❧ Diary entry March 10, 1984

How hard it is to be young! How very, very hard! I wonder why people always wish they were young again. Is it because old age is ugly or is it just that time effaces the hard chiseled outlines & leaves only the smooth hazy pastel picture? Youth, an ocean reflecting the sunrise and infested with deadly submarines; a stomach full of physics! God!

❧ Diary entry April 12, 1989 76th Birthday

I've been feeling depressed lately. The spa didn't help. I was feeling ok – sort of holding my own & people thought I was ok. But in me there is weeping.

❧ Diary entry July 16, 1990 6:15 AM

When I saw the Video CBC had done of me, I was absolutely enchanted.

Could this beautiful soulful lady, this caring, thoughtful, experienced, loving honest woman really be me?

I was in a trance about her.

How could I possibly bring her home to me, the me as I see myself, the me with all the blemishes, the aging woman I am today at 77?

(Yet I don't believe myself old and sexless.)

∾ Diary entry Aug 6, 1997 (age 84)

Well, another beginning, ten days before I leave for my trip on Regency Crown (on 17th), for Jewish Heritage 12 days cruise to Scandinavian countries, Helsinki and St. Petersburg. Hope I manage well. I'll wear my corset to keep my back firm and take along my walker – lots on my mind.

∾ Diary entry Aug. 12 1997

Hard to do everything alone, must attend to suddenly remembered details: wheelchair, Amer. extra cash, first or second sitting on ship, a question of visas to Petersburg, which clothes to take – will it be 65 degrees or warmer. Finally ironed 4 tops, got beige shoes fixed, haircut and tinting done, put most summer stuff away again. Now all clothes in living room. Final choices to be made. It's so hard...I do hope the sea air will give me a lift. My heart is very tired & I lie down a lot. Everything is a decision...walking gets harder. That area is good if one is well. I know I'm deteriorating & am more needy of help and don't know (trust) whom to ask. I remain "independent". So –

∾ Diary entry Feb 12, 1997

I need to continue to be seen and heard otherwise I will rot alone.

∾ Diary entry July 18, 2001 (age 88)

Funerals – so many funerals – columns & columns in the newspapers. My generation & younger people are moving on in truckloads to be buried. Most are really old – 80s and more. Endurance in the face of old age & disease has been lengthened. The "holding bins" – "residences" are crowded with deteriorated bodies & extinguishing spirits, waiting for the final <u>transport</u>.

Transport, that terrible word, which recalls the Holocaust. Yet all must die. In what manner? How lucky can you be? And what load of joy & anguish does each one drag along?

And when's my turn? My body pushes on – I wonder how. So much deterioration.

Last Golden Year

In October, 2000, Shulamis met a man who became the great love of her life. This love affair transformed her spirit and gave her a last golden year.

Her diary glows with the love, joy, and happiness she found.

This lover was a Renaissance man who combined business and writing; he was a well-rounded personality, avidly engaged with all the arts. She was eighty-seven and he was sixty-five. Although he lived in Western Canada and travelled extensively for his business, their time together was precious. In this late last relationship, Shulamis found what she had sought all her life: camaraderie and the excitement of being much in love with a soul mate. Their mutual love and affection energized both their lives.

❧ Diary entry June 11, 2002, Montreal General Hospital

Shulamis's last diary entry is an incomplete love poem, barely legible, written from her hospital bed shortly before she died:

"Betrothal Poem for D"

You said it was the longest night
And yet it was short for me
You walked in beauty in my sight –
A true epiphany

The garden woke, a golden glow
Though snow lay on the ground

You walked in beauty in my sight –
Though it was but a dream

Tues. Cont'd. 6 PM. 11/6/02
Tomorrow I'm to hear the decision of the
doctors — Rabinovitch, Charbonneau & the
chosen surgeon re if & when surgery.

8.30 PM.   Surprise
    Well, just had a call from Dr. Rab.
to say Dr. Verechenko had a cancellation
tonight & that he can take me at
noon to-morrow. Will I take it?
    His advice is Yes. And I've agreed.
If they think it Ok. I'll face the music
sooner & hopefully will heal sooner.
    I know its not going to be a
picnic, that the op. will probably take
up to 6 hours, then 24 hrs. in ICU &
if all's well, back here for the immediate
healing. It can take 3-6 mos!
    What choice have I got?
    The aneurism is growing again & there are
3 leakages should it burst I could die or experience
a terrible stroke. Rabinovitch says
to go ahead. He called Lilah & told her.
I don't want her to come now. She
should come later when she can be
of help. Now I must relax & pray for equilibrium.

Diary, June 11, 2002. Shulamis agrees to surgery. At 89 she was
in love and had a lot to live for.
Jewish Public Library

Death

Shulamis Borodensky Yelin died on June 22, 2002 at the Montreal General Hospital in her beloved city of Montreal, two weeks after suffering a fall and a subsequent heart attack. During her final days in hospital, Shulamis and her only child Gilah were reconciled and found peace together after so many years of extremely difficult relations.

"We were never closer," Shulamis whispered to Gilah during their last visit before her death.

Shulamis is buried in the cemetery of the Reconstructionist Synagogue. Gilah honoured her mother's explicit directions by inscribing her tombstone in the following way:

HEADSTONE

Shulamis Yelin
April 12, 1913 – June 22, 2002
I will say Yes to Life
Decision, *Seeded in Sinai*

FOOTSTONE

[Translated from the Hebrew]
Shulamis daughter of Vichna and Aaron Pheivel
Died 14th Tamuz, 5763   May her soul be bound in the cycle of life
Love is strong as death

SHULAMIS BORODENSKY YELIN
TEACHER, POET, AUTHOR
WIFE, MOTHER, SISTER
FRIEND

…but dull it never was! - sy

Véhicule Press
www.vehiculepress.com